UNFINISHED

UNFINISHED MISSION. UNFINISHED STORY.

BY

Vision for Latin America

Scripture References

All Scripture quotations are taken from the King James Bible.

Acknowledgements

We want to say a huge thank you to Shannon Penrod, who greatly assisted in the editing of this work. We would also like to extend our gratitude to Chris Fies and Trent Cornwell for their help on the cover design, as well as to the rest of our family at Vision Baptist Church and Vision Baptist Missions. Any souls that come to Christ as a result of this book's influence are undoubtedly fruit to your account.

TABLE OF CONTENTS

FOREWORD

It was 1999, and I was a nineteen-year-old college student on a six-month internship in Peru, South America. I was learning Spanish, trying new foods, and seeing things I had never seen. I had felt God wanted me to be a missionary since the time I was sixteen, but this was a whole new level. I was surrounded by people blindly dedicated to a Christless religion, unashamedly open immorality, and ever-present poverty. My eyes and heart were fully open; God was about to change my life forever!

I began to pray that God would allow me to see someone saved if He truly wanted me to be a missionary. I used my "Tarzan-like" Spanish to invite everyone I could to church, and finally someone came! It was a Sunday, and Germán, a young man who happened to be my neighbor, agreed to attend church with me. I was thrilled, and not long after, Germán was saved and baptized!

Within a short time, I was back in the U.S. finishing up Bible college. I began serving in the Spanish ministry there, and once again began to pray that God would allow me to see someone saved. I began inviting just about every Hispanic I met to church, all the while fervently praying that God would use me to lead another soul to salvation. I met Roberto, a seventeen-year-old Mexican who had not been in the U.S. for long. He began attending church with me, and soon he was both saved and baptized. God did it again!

I graduated from Bible college, and just a week later got married to my wife, Mindy. We raised our funds and headed to Latin America as missionaries, our first stop being Peru, to study the language and ministry under a veteran missionary, Austin Gardner. While on deputation and in language school, I began praying that God would start preparing the hearts of the Argentines to receive Him when I arrived. The day finally came, and I departed from language school to begin our first church in Buenos Aires, Argentina. My prayer changed to, "Now, God, would you send the Argentines whose hearts You have prepared?" And God once again answered our prayers! One by one, people began to come and receive Him as Savior. Young people began to surrender to serve God, and there was a need to start a Bible college where they could prepare for ministry. We saw marriages restored and lives changed. God was on the move. Soon another church and then another was launched! Young men were standing behind pulpits, and it was apparent that God was working in a very unique way.

I could share with you how a lady gave her own property to one of the churches and how God just laid a radio station right in our laps, but my aim is to simply prove to you that something special is happening in Latin America. God is working there. My story is one of many. Latin

America is a ripe harvest. While it is true that there are closed countries and difficult places around the world, Latin America seems to be in a prime season for missionaries to take the gospel there. I do not know how many more years the harvest will be ripe for reaping, but I do know that it is wide open right now. I plead with you, dear reader, would you give your life to take the gospel to Latin America? Would you take your proverbial bucket to Latin America and watch in amazement as God fills the bucket to overflowing? Would you simply pray, as I did so many years ago, "God, if you'll prepare the hearts and send them, I'll go gather them for you?" God is creating amazing waves of possibility in Latin America. Be one of the volunteers to go ride those waves!

Here to serve,
Jeffrey Bush
Director of Vision Baptist Missions

PREFACE

"It is finished!" Jesus cried on the cross as He gave His last breath.

There is something of finality to these words, as if a great feat had been accomplished. Indeed it had! In dying on the cross, Jesus completed the work that God the Father had given Him to do. All of us who know Him as Savior have that privilege because He didn't stop short of the finish line. He saw the work through to completion.

Shortly thereafter, He gave us a command known as the Great Commission. In Matthew 28:18-20, He directs us to preach the gospel to every creature. As you read this book, ask yourself this question: Can we truly say the job is complete in Latin America, and that there isn't more to be done?

We believe that as you read these pages, you will come to the realization that our work in Latin America is far from over. But simply knowing about a problem isn't the same as doing something about it. What is it that God wants you to do to reach Latin America with the gospel?

He has opened a great door there, and He expects us to step through it while there is still time. Let us not leave the mission...

Unfinished.

CHAPTER 1

Sacrifice

What if you were willing to give up everything?

Kevin White and Miguel Sanabria

Peter looked at Jesus, perplexed that He would suggest such a thing. To think that he could even consider denying the Lord in exchange for his own safety was preposterous. The other disciples, maybe, but Peter? No, he loved Jesus, had given his life to follow Him, and couldn't fathom a reason in the world why he should deny Him.

After all, hadn't he been the one who stood by Jesus when others had forsaken Him before? Hadn't he been the one who asked Jesus where they would go, because He had the words of eternal life? Wasn't he one of the three who were always with Jesus when something big was happening?

No, Peter would never deny Christ. And he would let it be known. "Though all men shall be offended because of thee, yet will I never be offended," he stated. *There, that settles it.*

But, strangely enough, instead of taking him at his word, Jesus singled Peter out as being the one who would deny Him three times before the cock crowed twice, before the night was even out. Peter couldn't believe his ears. "No!" His fist pounded the table, causing a few of the disciples to jump. "If I should *die* with thee, I will not deny thee in any wise."

And, true to his word, just moments later, when the soldiers came to take Jesus in the garden, Peter valiantly stood his ground and fought for Him, going so far as to strike off Malchus' ear. And yet Jesus didn't respond the way He was supposed to respond. Instead of joining the fight and defending Himself, He told Peter to put up the sword.

Peter must have been stunned. *This is not how this is supposed to go. You're supposed to fight with us. You're supposed to stop this from happening.* No doubt, he couldn't believe what he was seeing. Jesus was telling him to do something that went against everything in his nature. He was calling Peter to obey Him, no matter what Peter wanted. Peter had his own ideas, and Jesus Christ went completely against them.

When Jesus gave Himself up, everything changed. This was no longer a battle, this was complete surrender. At least, that's how it seemed to Peter, who did not know the rest of the story. And none of it made sense. Why would Christ ask him to do this?

Perhaps realizing what was happening, the disciples all forsook Jesus and fled. Somewhere along the way, though, Peter decided to follow at a safe distance to watch what would happen. But then even that plan went awry as people began to recognize him. Three times they asked if he was one of Jesus' disciples, and three times he denied it.

Irritated to the point of cursing at his questioners, he bellowed, "I know not the man!" Immediately, the cock crew, and Peter realized that Jesus had foretold the truth. Back when things were safe, and it was just Jesus and His disciples in a room together, declaring his loyalty to Jesus had come easily to Peter. But now, in the hour when it might cost him everything to be associated with Jesus Christ, in a time in which great sacrifice might be required to do so, he said, "I know not the man."

"I know not the man." Perhaps this all sounds familiar. Just like Peter, we're more than willing to follow Jesus as long as what He says and does makes complete sense to us. But as soon as He takes us in a direction we hadn't anticipated or that we wouldn't choose for ourselves, we too declare, "I know not the man."

We find ourselves getting comfortable with our life and our plans, then the Holy Spirit speaks to us through His

Word, a sermon, or a book, and says, "I want you to serve me on the mission field."

"But, Lord," we respond, "I have aspirations of my own."

I know not the man.

"I want you to give your whole life to me so that others may hear the gospel and be saved."

"Are you sure? My whole life? Is that really necessary?"

I know not the man.

"Your plans don't matter. Eternity is what matters. I gave my life so that others might be saved, and I want to use you to reach them."

"But what about the American Dream that I'm fighting so hard to attain? When will I achieve that?"

I know not the man.

We say we love Him, yet our lives betray us. Yes, we may go to church three times a week and give our tithes and offerings. We may do all these biblical things that the world would consider religious. But to sacrifice everything? To give our very lives for the gospel's sake, no matter what it costs? *Well,* we think, *let's not get too carried away.*

But perhaps that is just the thing Christ is calling you to do. Perhaps He is saying, "I don't want your things. I don't want your plans. I don't want your dreams. I want you. I want your life." Maybe He's been telling you that for some time now, or maybe you've picked up this book wondering: *Could God use me? And could He use me in Latin America?*

Yes, He can. B it will require complete surrender, and it will require sacrifice. But all the struggles we may face pale in comparison to this precious promise of Jesus: "Verily I say unto you, There is no man that hath left house, or parents, or brethren, or wife, or children, for the kingdom of God's sake, Who shall not receive manifold more in this present time, and in the world to come life everlasting," (Luke 18:29-30).

The Bible tells us that upon hearing the cock crow and seeing Jesus' knowing look, Peter went out and wept bitterly. No doubt his own words repeated themselves in his mind. *I swore I would go with him even unto death, and now look at me. I have my life, yes, but what is that worth now? I've denied the One I loved most.* How terrible his anguish must have been!

We read further that Jesus restored and forgave Peter, and that he went on to be used mightily of God. Wouldn't it be wonderful, though, if he had stood with Jesus all along, even when it didn't make sense? What heartache might he have escaped? What crushing guilt might he have avoided?

Peter died many years ago, and his story lives on in the pages of Scripture. In those same Scriptures, we see that Christ calls us to a life of sacrifice, even unto death, if so be. And yet, when called upon to give all for Jesus, so many of us echo these words along with Peter:

"I know not the man."

***

One area in particular that seems to be neglected when it comes to sacrificing everything is the Great Commission. Jesus told us in each of the Gospels and Acts to go into all the world and preach the gospel to every creature. His last command to us was to evangelize the world, yet that seems to be where so many have the biggest struggle surrendering to His will.

It is notable how many people give excuses for why they will not serve God on the mission field, and yet they would never offer up these same excuses for anything else. Were somebody to offer them 100 million dollars and say all they had to do was live in a foreign country and survive, they wouldn't say, "Well, it's too dangerous." Let's face it, most of them would say, "Well, for that amount of money, I'll take my chances!"

While it may seem harsh, I think we would all agree that is a fair assessment. Why is it that some are so willing to sacrifice for worldly things but not for something as important as God's will for their lives? Why are parents willing to let their kids move across the country to make a better salary, but complain about the distance when their child moves away to see souls rescued and brought into the kingdom of God? Why have Christians lost the idea of sacrificing all for God? I think there are a couple of things that might explain this:

We Don't See It As Our Responsibility

The first thing that should motivate us as believers to give our all and be willing to sacrifice everything is what we see in the Word of God. Many often say something like this: "If I only had the call of God on my life, I would be willing to go wherever He wanted." While they may be sincere, what they don't understand is that His call works first and foremost from His command. William Carey, the father of modern missions, said, "To know the will of God, we need an open Bible and an open map." So, instead of asking if it is God's will for us to be involved in world evangelism, we should be asking, "Where do I fit in God's plan for world evangelism?"

God's Word says, "Go."

"And he said unto them, Go ye into all the world, and preach the gospel to every creature..." (Mark 16:15).

First, we see the clear command for us to take the gospel to the whole world. Mark 16 states it as "every creature," leaving no doubt as to how far this command extends. Our main purpose in life, as we glorify God, is to take the good news of the gospel to those who have never heard.

Reconcile

"To wit, that God was in Christ, reconciling the world unto himself, not imputing their trespasses unto them; and hath committed unto us the word of reconciliation," (2 Corinthians 5:19).

One of the important aspects of obeying His command is to realize the ministry that has been given to us. If we have been reconciled (made right) to God through Christ, then we have also been given the ministry of reconciliation. We are the means that God uses to bring the lost to Him.

Those who don't know Christ are on the edge of death and separation from God, and we have the only gospel that can save them. As we see Christ's command and the ministry that has been given to us, we must be willing to sacrifice what is necessary to fulfill that command.

Forsake

"So likewise, whosoever he be of you that forsaketh not all that he hath, he cannot be my disciple," (Luke 14:33).

Many times when we look at a verse like this one, we try to run away from it or disregard its application to our life. Why is that? In this chapter, Jesus wants the people around Him to know what it takes to be His disciple. He tells them that they must put Him first and die to themselves daily. He tells them at the end that they must renounce everything in order to be His disciple.

When I (Miguel) first looked at these verses, I thought in my mind, *Wow, this is extreme, maybe a bit too much, maybe not for me.* At that time, I was still focused on what I had: my job, my money, my studies, my family, and everything I owned. I thought I was happy. I felt that all of these things were enough, but I soon found out that they would never satisfy me. My possessions became dated, my job was not stable, money was temporary, my family was crumbling, and everything I owned was never enough. Like so many who place their hopes in things of this world, I always wanted more.

Slowly, I started to realize that the One Who never changed was God, the One Who never broke His promises was Jesus, and the One Who never left me was the Holy Ghost. I began to realize that I was holding on to the wrong things in life. I knew that God had greater things for me than I had tried to acquire on my own.

In Luke 14:33, Jesus lays the terms of discipleship out for us so starkly that even the simplest of men can understand them. Those around Him knew what He was saying, hence why so many left. But look at all they missed out on when they did!

Have you ever thought about what it must have been like to witness Jesus heal a man who was blind? What about watching Him feed more than 5,000 people with just two fish and five loaves of bread? It must have been something out of this world. Can you imagine what the lives of Peter and John would have been like if they would not have forsaken everything and followed Jesus? They probably would have been fishermen for the rest of their lives. They would have died without having experienced all the events we read about in the book of Acts. But when they left everything to follow Christ, they stepped into a world full of impossibilities made possible. They accepted a life in which God would use them to do great and mighty things.

God wants the same for you. He wants to show Himself strong in your life. God does not want you to live perpetually tied to things that are always going to disappoint you. He wants to do the impossible with you. He wants you to let go of your world so that He can reach the world through you. God has such great things in store, but you must forsake all and follow Him.

We Don't See It As Our Priority

Another reason we may not sacrifice to serve God is because our priorities are out of order. This could be because some of us just don't care, but it could also be because we don't even realize it. Here are a couple of questions you can ask to assess if your priorities are where they should be:

Who Is First?

In our materialistic society, living a life-focused on "things" seems to be the norm. You might even seem strange if that isn't the focus of your life. The problem is that the Bible teaches us that God is a jealous God, and that if we want our lives to count as they should, He must be first. Matthew 6:33 says, "But seek ye first the kingdom of God, and his righteousness; and all these things shall be added unto you." Often well-intentioned people get this backwards. They think they must focus on the here and now, and if there is any time left, they will focus on the things of God. In this verse, the Bible not only teaches an important lesson, but also gives us an amazing promise. If we put God first in everything in our lives, He will provide for our every need. So ask yourself who is most important in your life. Whose dreams are you seeking, God's or yours? Where do you spend most of your time and effort? If it is not on the things of God, then you need to make some changes.

The Bible is clear that we can't serve God and this world at the same time. Matthew 6:24 says, "No man can serve two masters: for either he will hate the one, and love the other; or else he will hold to the one, and despise the other. Ye cannot serve God and mammon." The context here is money, but it definitely applies to anything that would challenge the place of Christ in our life. As Joshua said, we must decide whom we are going to serve and make that decision firm in our lives.

What Results Do You Want?

When you live for temporal things, the results that you get will be temporary as well. Not that they are necessarily sinful or wrong, but what you get will only last for this lifetime. If your priority is money and possessions, then you very likely will have money and possessions. But those things don't bring the happiness they promise. If you are looking for fame and position, you might be known and admired by many people. But in a hundred years, most likely no one will know who you were, and they probably won't care much if they do. At the end of your life, only what's done for Christ will last. I urge you, don't set up treasure on earth where it will decay, but in heaven, where it will last forever.

So what are the priorities in your life? I know that, as a Christian, deep down you want God to be first. But there is a battle raging that must be won. The self-desires and attractions of the world must be put to death. Make God and His work your priority, and you will begin to make a difference in this world that will last for all eternity.

We Don't See the Urgency of the Command

One last thing that will make a difference in our willingness to sacrifice all to reach the world with the gospel is realizing the urgency of the task. Since we have been working on the mission field, I (Kevin) have seen example after example that has confirmed God's hand in our being in Cochabamba, Bolivia. Some might ask, "Why should I sacrifice my life, plans, and dreams to go to another country and serve the Lord? Is it really worth it?" I want to share a couple of stories about what happened with us in Bolivia to show the urgency of reaching Latin America with the gospel.

The Last Flight

When we started our first church, we used English classes to try to make contact with as many people as possible and invite them to church. From those English classes we had about forty people who started coming to our first services. One of those families was the Arancibia family. Within the first few weeks, the whole family had made professions of faith. Not too long afterward, the wife's parents began to come and her father, César, got saved. They were a great family in the church, and he even started helping as an usher.

A couple of years later, we were preparing for our furlough, so we wanted to go by and see this family one last time before we left. At the end of the visit, I returned to my car and was about to leave when César came out and tapped on my window. He said he wanted to tell me something before I left. He began to tell me that when he was younger, he was a pilot, and on one of his trips they got into a terrible thunderstorm. He said that the plane was getting tossed about as they did everything possible to keep it in the air. At one point, it got so bad that the other pilot told him that if he needed to do anything to prepare for the end, right then would be the time to do it. He said that at that very moment, as death seemed imminent, it was as if the clouds opened and they could see the sun shining brightly through the opening. They were able to fly the plane toward that small window of hope and made it out of the storm alive.

As he stood by my car telling me this story, there were tears streaming down his face. He told me that for all those years he never understood why God had spared his life until he met us. He said that he realized that God spared his life so that he could hear the gospel and be saved. It was a great joy to see the mercy of the Lord and to know that we were able to have a part in taking the gospel to him and his family. A couple of months later, I got word that César had passed away from cancer. All I could think about was his taking that last flight and seeing his Savior face to face for the first time.

When I think about César and many others, I don't think it is a question of *if* we should go and sacrifice, but simply *when* and *where* we can go to make a difference in someone else's life.

The Right Place

When we were looking at starting our third church, we were praying about starting in an area called Pacata. There are about 50,000 people in that area and not one church that we knew of preaching the gospel. As we began to look for a place to plant a church, we drove up and down the main road asking in store fronts and looking in the newspaper for places to rent.

In the meantime, we started having services in the house of a man that would later become part of the church, but he lived a couple of miles outside of Pacata. For several months, we prayed and looked for the right place to start the church, but to no avail. At one point, I began to get frustrated and question God about why He wasn't opening the door for us to start the church in that area. I even began to doubt if it were the right area in which to start the church.

Later, I spoke with a friend who had lived in Pacata, and she told me that her neighbor was looking to rent her building. I didn't think it would lead to much but thought I would give it a try. When we met with her, she took us to her storefront, and I then realized that this was the very first door we had knocked on months ago with no answer. It was the perfect location, right at the main intersection of town. Not only that, but I began to see all along what the Lord had been doing. While we were at the man's house several miles up the road, his sister-in-law accepted Christ and began coming to church. Then, during one of our first youth meetings, the owner of our church building came and got saved. She was a strong Catholic, but it is now evident how God has changed her life. Once she came to me and said, "I am learning so many new things that I thought maybe I should bring a notebook to write them all down so I don't forget." I told her I thought that was an excellent idea.

The amazing thing about our ending up where we are is that several months prior, they were going to advertise the building for rent but decided not to, and just before they were going to put it in the newspaper, we called. So, while I was frustrated with God for not giving us a place to rent, He was using it all so that these people could get saved. If we had not gone to that area and trusted God's timing, then those people might not be saved today.

Go Before It Is Too Late

Unlike the previous two, this last story does not have a happy ending. Early in our first church plant, Eduardo and his family began to attend church because of the English classes that we were teaching. A couple of weeks later, during the invitation, they all raised their hands for salvation. Someone took them to the back and shared the gospel with them, and they trusted Christ as Savior.

Eduardo began helping as an usher in the church. During one of our conferences, we were standing outside because there were no more chairs available. He looked over at me and said, "This is all really amazing, what we now know, and the fact that we are saved." He then said, with tears in his eyes, "If only my dad would have been able to hear, I know he would have accepted it too." His father had passed away just a few months before we started the church. The only thing I could think was, *Why did we not get here a few months sooner?*

I know that God knows all these things and that we can't go back and change life, but it made me wonder how many other communities have people like Eduardo, whose

17

fathers are still alive and have time to hear and accept the truth if we will only go?

Is the sacrifice worth it? I think the answer is clear, and we must be willing to make that sacrifice *now* before it is too late.

What Led Me To Latin America

Stephen Carrier

"You can be anything you want to be, even president of the United States, if you set your mind to it and work hard." I heard these words growing up and took them directly to heart. President of the United States. Big dreams for a boy from a small city.

And yet those dreams of mine were real. Ever since I was a teenager, I knew that I was destined to be the next big thing in American politics. I came up with a plan to reach my goals and then pursued it with my whole heart.

Along the way, I got to work in a restaurant with a dishwasher named Enrique. Enrique was from Mexico, and he was my favorite dishwasher there because he was always so nice and just did his job. I was able to practice my high school Spanish with him and he would nod and laugh. Since I went to a small Christian school growing up, Enrique was really the first Spanish-speaking person with whom I came into frequent contact. I remember thinking how, if everybody from Latin America was like Enrique, then everybody from Latin America was fine by me.

19

Later, I had to take a couple of Spanish classes at my university, and one of the teachers challenged us to go to a Mexican restaurant and order off the menu in Spanish. I decided I was going to do that. As nervous as I was and as ridiculous as I felt, I managed to get the point across to the waiter. To my surprise, he actually liked it! The next thing I knew, I was friends with half the staff at that restaurant and others.

The Holy Spirit worked greatly in my heart over the next year or so, and I surrendered my life to Christ and foreign missions when I was twenty years old. Through various circumstances, God let me interact with several people from Latin America. I loved their friendliness and the way they treated me like family. There is still something so special about the way their faces light up when I begin to speak in Spanish to them. It wasn't long before I knew that this was the group of people God wanted me to reach for Him. These were my people, the ones God had given me to love. And how I do love them!

Ultimately, God has led me to Chile, but He could've taken me anywhere in Latin America and I would have absolutely loved it.

Maybe I could have been the president. But I know what I would've missed out on. I would've missed out on friendships with people from Latin America that are more valuable than money can buy. I would've missed out on learning a completely different culture full of people with open hearts who want to be a friend.

And I would've missed out on the opportunity to tell those same people about the Jesus I know and serve, Who can save them from their sins.

Did I sacrifice something to do what I'm doing? Maybe. But I wouldn't trade what I've gained for anything in this world.

Not even for being the president of the United States.

CHAPTER 2

Situation

What if you understood the conditions?

Shawn Bateman

It was an exciting age, an age of adventure and discovery. Ships laden with men and goods left the ports of Spain and Portugal and headed to the New World in search of treasure and places to establish new colonies. Priests traveled along with these adventurers. The conquest of South and Central America was not only a military campaign, but also a religious one as well. As the *conquistadors* made their way through the Americas, so did Catholicism. The missionaries who accompanied them had the challenge of converting the indigenous population to the practices of the Catholic faith, as well as teaching them how to live in a new society under the rule of the Europeans.

In 1513, the Spanish King Ferdinand II of Aragon signed the "Requerimiento," or the "Requirement." This document declared the divine right of Spanish rule and their intentions for the native populations. While there had been laws enacted earlier to prevent the mistreatment of the native populations, the "Requerimiento," through political maneuvering and religious jargon, side-stepped many of these issues, legitimizing war, slavery, and death if the native peoples resisted. The people of Latin America had to accept missionaries in their presence and submit to all Spanish authority. Though the document didn't call for forced conversion, the population of the Americas really had two options: convert to Catholicism and submit to Spanish rule, or suffer the deadly consequences. So began the centuries-long domination of Catholicism over Central and South America.

Much of the time the native peoples of the Americas incorporated Catholicism into their own religions, traditions, and superstitions. The result would be a Catholicism very different than that which was practiced across the Atlantic. It was important that they practiced their new-found "faith" in such a way that satisfied their priests and their overlords. Even today, this mixing of Catholicism and superstition is found all throughout Latin America. A good example of this is "Nuestra Señora de la Santa Muerte," which is literally translated "Our Lady of Holy Death." Many times it is shortened to "Santa Muerte." It is believed that this devotion to death has evolved from pre-Colombian times, and even though it is condemned by the Catholic Church, it has been practiced for centuries, ever growing in popularity. A friend of mine told me that he recently became aware that a lady who had been attending his church for years prays and burns incense to an idol to Santa Muerte that she keeps in her home.

While the Protestant Reformation was taking place in Europe and completely changing the landscape of most of the countries, the two countries that would hold sway and control basically all of Central and South America, Portugal and Spain, saw very little influence from the Reformation. The first evangelical missions activity in Latin America was from a group of French Huguenots escaping Catholic persecution. With the help of many Huguenot leaders from France and the reformer John Calvin from Geneva, they attempted to establish a colony in Brazil. Five years later, the Portuguese had extinguished this first glimmer of light in South America. The governments of Portugal and Spain vehemently resisted the Reformation and would not tolerate anything that was not Catholic. As a result, there were little to no religious freedoms found in Latin America for centuries.

As citizens of the U.S., it can be difficult for us to put into perspective the great privileges that have been afforded to us. Some of our first colonies were established as a haven where people could worship according to the dictates of their conscience, free from fear of persecution. Long before our independence was won, our country was established on a foundation of religious liberty. This mindset did not exist in Latin America. Following on the heels of America's war for independence from England, much of Latin America engaged in their own war for independence from Portugal and Spain. Just like the United States, Latin America has its own heroes of revolution. Generals San Martín and Simon Bolívar helped liberate what is now Argentina, Chile, Paraguay, Uruguay, Bolivia, Peru, Colombia, Venezuela, and Ecuador. A priest named Father Miguel Hidalgo helped start the fires of independence in Mexico, and Dom Pedro I of Brazil, who was the son of the Portuguese king, set Brazil free from Portugal. While the war for independence in the U.S. solidified religious freedom for all, in Latin America it only opened the door for religious liberty to begin to enter. The coming of independence was accompanied by a wave of non-Catholic immigrants and missionaries. Catholicism started to lose its dominating power, but it was a slow and painful process.

The Spreading of the Gospel in Latin America

The stories of the first missionaries to work in Latin America are tales of great triumph and hardship. Though not as well-known as their contemporaries William Carey, Adoniram Judson, and David Livingstone, these Latin American missionaries are nonetheless heroes of the faith.

The first missionary to leave North America for Latin America was a freed slave named George Liele. Liele was born in Virginia and was later taken to the state of Georgia, where he was born again in 1773 and began to preach the gospel.

Toward the end of the American Revolutionary War, his master set him free. Liele had sided with the British during the war, and as a Loyalist he was able to move his family to Jamaica with the intent of starting Baptist churches there. This took place more than a decade before William Carey would set out to India as a missionary. Liele worked hard as a bi-vocational minister, and there were more than 8,000 conversions attributed to his ministry there. Years later, the Baptist churches in Jamaica would be a strong force in sending missionaries throughout Latin America.

Some of the first evangelical communities formed in Latin America came as a result of immigration. In the 1850's, Uruguay and Argentina received groups of Waldensian immigrants. There was substantial immigration in the 1860's from Wales to the Argentinian Patagonia, bringing Methodists, Baptists, Anglicans, and Congregationalists. Each of these immigrant groups met with fierce persecution from the Catholic Church and community. The Jesuit priests especially fought to persecute these groups and contain them from spreading. As a result, these immigrant communities did very little to help spread the gospel, but rather became closed-off communities.

On other occasions, missionary activity was initiated as a result of the immigrant population. Baptists and Methodists would send missionaries to begin churches found in some of these English communities. Methodist missionaries became some of the first missionaries to learn Spanish and to begin preaching and doing ministry in Spanish. One example was the Methodist missionary Fountain Pitts, who arrived in 1835 as the official emissary of American Methodists. He was assigned to explore the possibilities of starting a Methodist work in the River Plate Republics and Brazil. Pitts was able to build up the work in his short time in Buenos Aires and make it principally a Methodist endeavor. He returned to the US in 1836, and as a result of his report, the Methodists sent a very capable missionary, John Dempster, to further the Methodist Mission. Dempster's effective ministry sparked the beginning of the Methodist denomination in Argentina and Uruguay. Years later, the Methodists, who had begun evangelizing in Spanish, were very helpful to the first Baptist missionaries.

War sometimes played a role in the spread of the gospel. For example, during Cuba's Ten Years' War from 1868-1878, many Cuban patriots were exiled to the United States. One of these patriots was Albert Díaz. He was converted in a Baptist church in New York City, returned to his native country in 1882, and there organized a congregation. Three years later, he was ordained as a Baptist minister and led his church into becoming a Baptist congregation.

Another story of how war moved the gospel into Latin America is that of James Hickey. Hickey was an

Irishman who was studying to become a priest in the Catholic church. He was disgusted by the immorality of the clergy, so he left off studying and married a young Lutheran girl. Upon hearing clear gospel teaching, Hickey was converted and began to study for the ministry again in the Anglican church. Due to disagreements in doctrine, he became a Baptist. After the death of his wife, he moved to Canada and then to the United States, working as a bi-vocational minister for a number of years. He later remarried, and in 1861, at the onset of the American Civil War, he found himself in Texas. Hickey was a strong abolitionist and would have nothing to do with war, so he moved south of the border and began to preach in Mexico. Baptists in Mexico claim Hickey as their founder, as he started the first Baptist congregation there.

Fredrick Crowe was one of the least-expected missionaries in Latin American history. Crowe was a well-educated, but very rebellious young man. He left his home bound for Guatemala, but because of his bad conduct aboard ship, he was left in Belize in 1836. An English Baptist missionary who was ministering in the area was able to win this rebellious young man to the Lord. Because of his education, he was eventually invited to teach as a schoolmaster, and he used the Bible as his primary textbook. In 1841, the Baptists in Belize commissioned him as a missionary. He began to open schools throughout Guatemala and to preach and evangelize in the capital city. Crowe was very popular among the young people, but the conservative government saw his evangelizing practices as a threat and kicked him out of the country. He penned a book entitled The Gospel in Central America to document his ministry.

Allen Francis Gardiner (1794-1851) deserves a prominent place among the intentional pioneers of Latin America. He joined the British navy at sixteen, a strong, athletic young man who distinguished himself in seamanship and combat. He reached the rank of commander after serving in the Napoleonic Wars and various forays into South America. He was saved during this time, and it brought about a deep and profound change in his life. While in Chile in 1822, he came into contact with some indigenous peoples and was deeply moved to dedicate his life to reaching the abandoned peoples of the earth with the gospel. In the 1840's, and until his death, Gardiner worked at trying to establish missions among the natives in Patagonia. He eventually starved to death along with his whole group in 1851 after supplies failed to reach them.

James Thompson is credited with introducing the Baptist denomination to most Latin American countries. Thompson was a Scottish pastor before launching into a career in missions. He arrived in Buenos Aires on October 6, 1818, as a representative of the Foreign Bible Society. He worked in the capital as an educator until 1821. During this time, he imported Spanish New Testaments to be used as textbooks. Though he had the support of the educators in Argentina, the Catholic clergy was suspicious of him and had him under constant observation.

Thompson left Argentina and headed to Chile in 1821, and the authorities honored him with citizenship before he left. The public school systems in Chile, Peru, and Argentina were pioneered by Thompson. He left Chile in 1822 and moved on to Peru, where he met José San Martín, the great military leader who is known as "The Liberator." San Martín was impressed with Thompson's system and helped promote Thompson's ministry.

Along with Bible distribution and education, Thompson also helped start work on Bible translations in various native languages throughout South America. Thompson's ministry ranged from South America to the Caribbean and North America. Given the many restrictions placed on missionaries at the time, Thompson's goal wasn't necessarily to proselytize, but to stir up interest in the gospel throughout the New World. His ministry in North and South America came to an end in 1842 because of an illness. He went back to Europe, where he visited North Africa and helped the Spaniards fight for religious freedom. He died in 1855, having lived a most extraordinary life.

Religious Freedom

The story of the spread of the gospel in Latin America is also the story of religious freedom. Gospel preachers were persecuted and jailed. Protestants were prohibited from evangelizing or holding public services. Countries like Argentina that had a higher immigrant-based society experienced religious freedom more quickly than other countries like Peru and Bolivia.

One man who helped greatly with religious liberty was Francisco Penzotti (1851-1925), who emigrated from Italy to Uruguay at the age of thirteen. Upon reading the New Testament, he became an evangelical Christian. He developed his ministry under the tutelage of Dr. Thomas Wood from the Methodist church in the city of Montevideo. From 1883 to 1906, Penzotti traveled by ship, mule, foot, and whatever other means necessary, from Chile all the way to Mexico, opening offices for the American Bible Society and starting churches. On January 10, 1889, in El Callao, a harbor near Lima, Peru, Penzotti founded the first evangelical church officially established in the country, the Iglesia Metodista Episcopal del Callao. Afterward, Penzotti spent eight months in a Peruvian prison, accused of preaching a different faith than the official one. Immediately after his imprisonment, the country became torn by civil strife between the allies and enemies of Penzotti, an uproar so intense that it reached the highest officials. This episode was instrumental both in changing the country's laws to allow freedom of religion and in opening the country to the gospel.

Catholicism's hold is still very strong. In many countries, the Catholic Church still receives support from the government in funds as well as in preferential treatment. For years, Protestants were denied the ability to serve their country in public office. For example, the Argentine president was required by constitutional law to be a Roman Catholic until 1994, when this requisite was overturned.

Today there is religious freedom throughout Latin America. In some cases, there are perhaps more religious freedoms in Latin America than in the United States. Currently in Latin America, the only real threat to religious freedom is found in Communism and Socialism. Cuba and Venezuela have stopped missionary activity in their countries, and there are concerns at times that Bolivia's government will interfere in religious affairs. Aside from these examples, Latin America enjoys great religious liberties. An open door stands before this generation of missionaries. It was a door that was forced open by brave men and women willing to risk it all for the gospel.

Latin America Today

Things in Latin America have changed drastically in the last fifty years. Forty percent of all the Catholics in the world live in Latin America. Just fifty years ago, 90% of adults in Latin America identified as Catholic, a number that has fallen to 69% today. At present, nearly one in five adults in Latin America claims Protestantism. In recent surveys, those who have turned from the Catholic faith to Protestantism most frequently cite that they are looking for a more personal connection with God.

Folk Catholicism is still practiced, as well as certain folk religions unique to their own countries or regions. Voodoo is still practiced in Haiti; Winti and Javanism are still practiced in Suriname. People pray to Santa Muerte throughout Latin America, and in Argentina the red shrines of El Gauchito Gil can be seen along the interstates. Latin America is a very superstitious culture, and though these different folk religions hold a small percentage of the population today, that grasp is still incredibly strong.

The Mormons and Jehovah's Witnesses are growing throughout Latin America. In every major city, Jehovah's Witnesses are present, passing out their literature, and they have consistently grown over the last 100 years. The Mormons have experienced a huge increase of over 500% growth over the last forty years.

Pentecostalism has considerable influence in Latin America. It was brought in by the Pentecostal missionaries in the early 20th century, but quickly became Latinized. The faith healing and emotionally-charged services appealed to the Latin American culture. One prominent denomination, the Assemblies of God, first sent out missionaries to Brazil in the early 20th century. Today there are between two and three million Assemblies of God congregants in the United States, but there are over twelve million in Brazil.

Among the many concerns of practice and doctrine that we might have with Pentecostalism, the most troubling is the prosperity gospel that they promote. Throughout Latin America, the prosperity gospel is proclaimed to millions of people each week. People hear this message of how they can come out of their poverty if they will give generously to the church. This message is attractive to Latin Americans because of the high poverty that is found in most of its countries.

Latin America is very religious and "Christianized" in one sense. Often people can be seen praying in public at shrines to the Virgin Mary or other saints. Many talk about the church that they go to in order to be healed, liberated, or to receive blessings of prosperity. However, very few, if any of them, when questioned about salvation, can give a response that remotely looks like the gospel.

There is still much to do in Latin America. The new missionaries, pastors, and churches will not face the persecutions that many faced 200 years ago, but they will face new challenges. What was needed then is still needed now: visionary men and women who have the imagination and

resolve to get the message of salvation to the masses in Latin
America.

What Led Me To Latin America

Tracy Paver

"Your reasonable service." I stared at those three words in my Bible, overcome by their meaning. I was at a missions camp in the mountains of Tennessee. I had just graduated from nursing school the month before and figured this camp would be a welcome hiatus before I dove back into the world of nursing, NCLEX-RN exam preparation, and job interviews. But after the first camp service, I knew this wasn't going to be the low-stakes, relaxing camp I'd imagined. A missionary preached on Romans 12:1, challenging us to surrender to missions and serve Jesus with our lives. It left me feeling uncomfortable, unsettled.

Because of an American missionary who shared the gospel with my dad in the Philippines, I had the blessing of growing up in a Christian home and getting saved at the age of seven. God would later move my family to Singapore and Indonesia, where I made a diverse group of friends, many of whom were missionary kids. The move overseas made me more aware of my spiritual surroundings, the false teachings of Hinduism, Buddhism, and Islam, and the world's great need for the gospel. But the move also helped me understand in part what it was like for a missionary to leave the comfort, familiarity, and security of home to live in a foreign land, to adapt to culture, to learn a language, and to share the gospel with people in darkness. Living overseas, seeing the gospel need, and counting missionary kids as some of my closest friends helped keep my heart open toward missions.

"But, Lord," I thought, "You can't possibly want me to surrender in this way. Not yet. It's too early." I had just finished a challenging four-year nursing program. I was at the beginning of what I hoped would be a long, successful career, either in cardiac or orthopedic nursing at some prestigious teaching hospital in the South. There would be plenty of time for missions later. But that week at camp, I couldn't get that phrase out of my mind: "Your reasonable service." "Reasonable" meaning rationale and sensible. As I meditated on Romans 12:1, I realized that giving my life to serve Jesus isn't an excessive or extreme act. It is a rationale, reasonable response when I consider whom I was before salvation, Whom God is, and what He sacrificed to save me.

Still, I held back, wondering if I could really trust God with the surrender of my life. I was afraid of where surrender would take me, of the kind of life I would have. But it was another verse in Romans that quieted the fear in my heart. "He that spared not his own Son, but delivered Him up for us all, how shall he not with him also freely give us all things?" (Romans 8:32). God had given me His very best, His most beloved Son, "that whosoever believeth in Him should not perish but have everlasting life." That's a good God. That's an *immeasurably gracious and kind God. That's a God I can trust with my life. On the last night of camp, I gave up my plans for the reasonable service of giving my life to serve the Lord as a missionary.*

When I look back on that missions camp and how God worked in my heart, I am overwhelmed by His goodness. All I wanted was a week-long break from studying for the NCLEX-RN exam, but God wanted to work something else out in my life that was of far greater value. Since camp, I learned to prioritize my life differently. Instead of letting a job dictate my direction, I moved to Alpharetta, Georgia, because of a pastor, church, and missions training program. There I knew I could get discipled, mentored, and trained for missions and ministry. I learned to balance studying at the Our Generation Training Center and serving at Vision Baptist Church while working at a local hospital and teaching in various nursing programs. I learned to be willing to serve in different capacities. And I learned, and am still learning, to be sensitive to the Lord's leading.

God used a recent missions trip to Latin America to open my eyes to the continued need for the gospel in this region. He also showed me what He could do through the lives of faithful men and women wholly surrendered to Him. What my eyes saw affected my heart, and I began to pray and search for an opportunity to serve. And that's when God directed my steps to Chile, a country that, despite its still predominant

Catholicism and growing population of atheists and agnostics, is ripe for the harvest.

Long before I stepped onto Latin American soil and saw the gospel need, before I even started deputation as a missionary to Chile, God was already at work in my heart. And it began with the realization that giving my life to serve Jesus isn't an excessive or extreme response. It is simply my reasonable service.

CHAPTER 3

Statistics

What if you saw the people in Latin America as more than just numbers?
Daniel Sparks

I grew up in a wonderful pastor's home outside of Atlanta, Georgia. Every year my family and I would visit our relatives who lived in the hills of Knoxville, Tennessee, for Christmas and for a summer family reunion. I had also traveled to other neighboring states like Alabama, Florida, Kentucky, and the Carolinas. However, I had never left the southeastern United States until I went on my first mission trip in the summer of 2001 after graduating from high school at the age of eighteen.

I remember loading up an old bus that belonged to our church early one morning with my youth group and heading for the Mexican border along Texas. We got on Interstate 20 and headed due west through Alabama, Mississippi, Louisiana, and finally to Texas. While in Texas, right outside of Dallas, our church bus overheated and decided it had had enough. We had to pull over to the side of the interstate to check it out. In the blazing hot summer sun, many of us were asked to get out and help push the large bus to a nearby mechanic shop. I remember that being the hottest, most miserable day I had ever experienced in all my eighteen years of life. Nothing but black, burning hot asphalt and sweaty hands, pushing a scalding hot metal bus for what seemed like an eternity.

My first day spent outside of the Southeast was a memorable one, but for several unpleasant reasons. The mechanics did manage to get the bus fixed, and after driving what seemed like a dozen more hours, we made it to the Mexican border. At the border, we met some American missionaries who picked us up in a yellow school bus. We made it past border patrol and traveled another four hours or so through the dry, barren desert before we reached the city of Jiménez.

While in Mexico, I noticed a startling difference. All over the southeastern United States, there were gospel-preaching churches galore! In Jiménez, meanwhile, there were about 50,000 people, with only one independent Baptist church. There were other similar-sized cities also without churches preaching sound doctrine. We visited villages that had never seen any minister of any kind. Many had never even seen a Bible before. The vast majority had nobody to share the gospel with them. Upon seeing all of this, I became burdened for the people.

It was there, in Mexico, where I surrendered my life to be a Spanish-speaking missionary to Latin America. I could not think of any greater thing I could do with my life than to tell others about Jesus. I knew how blessed I was to be a part of a great church that taught biblical truths and showed the love of Christ to others. I wanted the same for the people of Latin America. I knew God could use me to reach the multitudes outside the borders of the United States for His glory.

Population of Multitude

Latin America has a population of over 650 million people, which is approximately one-tenth of the world's population. The region is made up of 20 countries and 13 dependencies stretching across the continents of North and South America. Latin America stretches from the northern border of Mexico and the Caribbean islands to the southern tip of Chile. It consists of nearly double the land area of the U.S., with nearly double the population.

There are four commonly referred to subregions of Latin America: North America, Central America, the Caribbean, and South America. Mexico is the only North American country considered to be a part of Latin America. Central America is made up of Guatemala, Belize, El Salvador, Honduras, Nicaragua, Costa Rica, and Panama. The Caribbean subregion is made up of a host of small island countries and dependencies, including Cuba, the Dominican

Republic, Haiti, and Puerto Rico. The subregion of South America would make up all the countries and dependencies on the continent of South America. The term Latin America is sometimes used more broadly to refer to all of the Americas south of the U.S.

The term "Latin America" was first used in 1856 by the Chilean politician Francisco Bilboa in Paris, France, during a political conference. Today the term generally refers to territories in the Americas where Spanish, Portuguese, French, and Creole languages are spoken. These languages are derived from Latin and are also considered Romance languages. Therefore, Latin America is defined as the parts of the Americas that were once parts of Spanish, Portuguese, and French Empires.

Brazil is the sixth most populated country in the world, and with 211 million people, has by far the highest population among Latin American countries. The second most populous country in Latin America is Mexico with 127 million people. Colombia has the third highest population with 50 million inhabitants, followed by Argentina with 45 million, Peru with 32 million, and Venezuela with 28 million. There are nine other Latin American countries with a population of more than 10 million people.

Population of "Christians"

About 90% of the people of Latin America claim to be Christian. About 69% of those claiming to be Christian identify with the Catholic religion. Protestants make up about 17% of the Christian population in Latin America. However, the Protestant population is much higher in Central America and Brazil, at 44% and 26% respectively.

You might be thinking that 90% of Latin Americans identifying themselves with Christianity is extremely high. You would be absolutely correct. For example, the United States claims to be a Christian nation, but only 65% of Americans identify as being Christian. Although the vast majority of the United States claims to be Christian, as does Latin America, we as American believers who have done any kind of personal evangelism know that almost 3 out of every 4 people are not truly believers.

We should define the word "Christian." In the Bible, the words "Christian" or "Christians" are only mentioned three times, twice in Acts and once in 1 Peter. It has to do with a radically different way of living (Acts 11:26, 26:28) and is associated with suffering and not being ashamed (1 Peter 4:16). The 90% of Latin Americans who identify themselves as Christians do not conduct themselves in a manner worthy of being labeled a Christian. Just because someone says they are a Christian does not really mean they are. People today use the word very frequently and erroneously. Anyone can call themselves a Christian, but really it is a term that others should use about a person because they are exemplifying Christlike virtues and living a radical lifestyle, in comparison to the world, for the glory of God.

A true believer in Christ has first heard, received, believed, and been saved (1 Corinthians 15:1-3) by the message of "the gospel of the grace of God," (Acts 20:24). Paul assured his Galatian brothers in Christ that he did not receive this gospel by man, nor was he taught it, "but by the revelation of Jesus Christ." The gospel message that Paul preached was "that Christ died for our sins...and that he was buried, and that he rose again the third day," (1 Corinthians 15:3-4). Many of the people of Latin America have heard this gospel message. However, the vast majority of the so-called Christian churches add good works and other requirements to the message of the gospel of grace to obtain or maintain one's salvation. Ephesians 2:8-9 tells us, "For by grace are ye saved through faith; and that not of yourselves: it is the gift of God: Not of works, lest any man should boast." The gospel message of God's free gift of salvation is by His grace through faith in Jesus Christ alone, not by any work or righteousness of our own. Henceforth, it would certainly be a stretch to say that 90% of Latin Americans are truly saved, born-again Christians, because they are being taught that they have to work to secure their salvation. What is being taught in the vast majority of churches is that Jesus' sinless life and undeserved death on the cross for the sins of the entire world is not enough to save any single person from an eternity in the lake of fire.

Latin America is filled with Christian churches and the Christian religion. Unfortunately, there is only a small amount of solid Bible-teaching, Bible-preaching churches. I would say that the Bible is our sole and final authority on all matters of faith and practice. On the contrary, the majority of Christian churches in Latin America would teach from the Bible but would also use other non-inspired books and doctrines in addition to the Bible, while belittling the Bible and rejecting it as the sole authority on all matters. The Bible says in 2 Timothy 3:16 that, "All scripture is given by inspiration of God, and is profitable for doctrine, for reproof, for correction, for instruction in righteousness." I have decided to only trust the Bible, which is the written Word of God, and I will judge every other book I read based on the Bible because it alone is truth (John 17:17; Colossians 1:5; 1 Thessalonians 2:13).

Understanding Our Focus: Why We Go to Cities

We go to large cities for many reasons. The most obvious reason would be because that is where the greatest number of people are located. The more people there are, the more opportunities arise to share the gospel with others.

The world urbanization rate has been on a steady rise since the 1950's. At the turn of the 20th century, just 15% of the world population lived in cities. According to the United Nations, the year 2007 witnessed the turning point when more than fifty percent of the world's population was living in cities for the first time in human history.

Urbanization occurs for various reasons. Living in a city can be culturally and economically beneficial. It can provide greater opportunities for access to the job market, better education, housing and safety conditions, and reduce the time and expense of commuting and transportation. Conditions like density, proximity, diversity, and marketplace competition are all elements of an urban environment that attracts people. In cities, money, wealth, services, healthcare, and opportunities are all centralized. Cities offer a larger variety of services, including specialist services not found in rural areas. These services require workers, resulting in more numerous and varied job opportunities. Elderly people may be forced to move to cities where there are doctors and hospitals that can cater to their health needs. High-quality educational opportunities are another factor in urban migration, as well as the opportunity to join, develop, and seek out social communities. It is also easier for women to find employment and have access to education in an urban setting.

Over the past 45 years, Latin American cities have boomed. In 1950, 40% of the region's population was urban, but today, over 82% live in cities, making Latin America the world's most urbanized region. By 2050, UN-Habitat predicts Latin America's cities will include 90% of the region's population.

The Apostle Paul's missionary journeys followed a pattern of preaching and planting churches in cities that were central and influential. From these cities, the message of the gospel could spread throughout the province. Paul focused on specific metropolitan cities that could strategically reach other cities, villages, and towns. His goal did not seem to be planting a church that would become big and important like the megachurches we see today. Instead, he planted churches that would plant more churches in the surrounding areas. Paul's intention was to have the church situated in the city to be a center of light for the whole province. He chose to plant churches in areas of higher influence, and these churches had strong potential for long-term influence in particular provinces. Although there is nothing wrong with someone's planting a church in a small village, Paul's methodology is a biblical model that should be considered. There is much wisdom in understanding his church-planting strategy, knowing he followed the leading of the Holy Spirit in his ministry (Acts 16:6-7; Acts 21:4).

Another reason why we go to larger, strategic cities is that young people and young families are drawn to the cities. They can find jobs more easily. They can get a fresh start on their own. Young people enjoy the amenities of the city. In the city, you don't have to go searching for youth behind closed doors. They are out and about, walking on the sidewalk, hanging out with friends in the park, being adventurous and trying to figure out just where they fit into life.

As a church-planting missionary, I am always looking for young, influential, teachable men whom I can train in the ministry so that they, too, can train other leaders. Paul gave some really valuable advice to Timothy about this subject. He said, "And the things that thou hast heard of me among many witnesses, the same commit thou to faithful men, who shall be able to teach others also," (2 Timothy 2:2). Typically, the younger a person is, the more they will listen to you. If they will listen, they can be influential and trainable. If you attempt to train someone who has already "been there, done that," the chances of their willingness to learn is less likely.

Another thing I have noticed about church planting in a large important city is that there are a lot of people from other cities and countries that have come looking for opportunities. I have the great privilege to serve the Lord in Santiago, Chile. Santiago is the capital city of Chile, and, by extension, the most important and largest city as well. It is strategically located in the center of Chile's long, narrow strip of land. In our current church plant that is less than a year old, at any given church service we will have up to seven different nationalities represented. In fact, the majority of our people are not Chilean. They are from other Latin American countries. Some have lived in Santiago for more than 20 years. Others have only lived here for less than a couple of years. Most have come to our city to seek opportunities and a better way of living for themselves and their families.

When people relocate to a new city, they are usually looking to make new friends and are open to new things. Everything is new to them and they are away from their comfort zone. They are trying to fit in and trying to be accepted. A church is an ideal place for them to meet new people. We have had so many visitors that fit this way of thinking, who are willing to venture out beyond their normal boundaries.

The Most-Populated Latin American Cities Compared to American States

There are about 70 metropolitan cities in Latin America with populations of more than one million people.

In comparison, there are over 50 U.S. metropolitan cities with more than one million people.

If we are going to reach Latin America with the gospel, we should strongly consider the metropolitan cities as starting points. We could start a church in these cities, reach people, train them in the ministry, and then send them out to other nearby cities. If the Lord allowed me to train just ten faithful men during my time in the ministry, and those ten men each trained ten more, during my lifetime there could be a potential of 1,000 faithful gospel messengers to start 1,000 more gospel churches!

A ministry goal I have on my heart is to see at least one church planted for every 50,000 people. In Santiago, where I live and minister, we still need about 140 churches to make this goal a reality. This is an attainable goal if we continue faithfully training men for the ministry. In all of Latin America, we would need a total of 13,000 churches in order to have one church per 50,000 people. Would you pray with us for laborers?

But even more, would you consider going to Latin America as a missionary to accomplish this task?

Below is a chart of the top 10 largest metropolitan cities in Latin America, along with their population and U.S. state comparison in population. Please pray with us about the evangelization of these 10 strategic cities, for more men to be trained, and for more churches to be planted.

City	Metro Population	Comparison
São Paulo, Brazil	22 million	Florida
Mexico City, Mexico	21.7 million	Florida
Buenos Aires, Argentina	15.1 million	Pennsylvania
Rio de Janeiro, Brazil	13.4 million	Illinois
Bogata, Colombia	10.8 million	Georgia
Lima, Peru	10.6 million	North Carolina
Santiago, Chile	6.8 million	Tennessee
Belo Horizonte, Brazil	6 million	Missouri
Guadalajara, Mexico	4.9 million	Alabama
Monterrey, Mexico	4.7 million	Louisiana

What Led Me To Latin America

Robert Becker

When I surrendered to missions, Latin America was not on my radar at all. I had my own plans, actually, but in 2017, my wife and I took a missions trip to Peru with our pastor. While there, he showed us around the ministry in Arequipa, Peru. The Lord started speaking to me about considering South America, but I still told Him that I had my own plans about where I wanted to go.

In January 2018, my wife and I were given the opportunity to spend six months in Buenos Aires, Argentina, with missionary Patrick Henry. While we were there, we got to help out in his church plant as well as visit different parts of the city. We saw a statue where people left ashes of their deceased loved ones and prayed to the statue for their souls. These people had been lied to about Whom Jesus really is. They believe in a Jesus who tells them they have to work their way to heaven. They do not know about the true Jesus Who already paid the price for their sins and wants them to accept His free gift of salvation. This really broke our hearts and the Lord began working on us. We started praying about what He would have us to do.

I can remember going all around the metro Buenos Aires area with its nearly 14 million inhabitants. Buenos

Aires has a very good train system, and I used the train nearly every day with thousands of people crammed into this tiny space, barely able to breath, and feeling like we could suffocate from the heat. One day, as I was squished into this small area unable to move anything except my head, I looked around on the train and saw all these people. I thought to myself that, if they have not believed on the name of the only Son of God, they are all condemned already, as John 3:18 says. These are people's fathers, mothers, sons, and daughters. I can remember thinking that many of them would go to hell, as many have not heard the true gospel of Jesus Christ. I looked past the numbers and saw the people who have hopes and dreams and are striving for a better life, but will be unable to find it without Jesus Christ.

At one point, I mentioned to Patrick that there was a real lack of Bible-believing, Bible-preaching churches in Buenos Aires. And he responded in a way I'll never forget. He asked, "What are you going to do about that, Robert?" His question haunted me as I pondered God's direction for my life.

One day I woke up, and the still small voice of the Lord told me, "I want you here, Robert. Come back to Argentina and tell these people what I have done for them." It was then that I surrendered myself to return to plant churches and to train men to continue in the ministry.

When you think of Latin America, do not simply think of the masses of people, but see their individual souls that are lost and in need of a Savior. And ask yourself, as I did, "What am I going to do about it?"

CHAPTER 4

Shift

What if you changed your way of thinking?

Patrick Henry and Jonathan Anderson

"Is the name of Jesus enough?"

I (Patrick) stood in front of our young church and asked this very question. Most did not know how to answer. In Argentina and in most of Latin America, almost everyone knows the name of Jesus. They have heard it in school, seen it on Catholic Church signs, and observed statues of Jesus as a baby and as a man. The name of Jesus is known, but is it enough?

If people were saved just by hearing and knowing the name of Jesus, Latin America and many other places would be completely reached. In fact, we could evangelize the world simply by renting out signs in places of business, airing commercials during important events, and proclaiming His name on the giant screens of stadiums during sports games. But the truth is that the name of Jesus isn't enough. Just to hear and know His name does not save anyone. If someone dies knowing the name of Jesus and another dies not knowing the name of Jesus, they will both go to the same lake of fire. There is no benefit to having heard the name "Jesus."

That is not to say that the name of Jesus isn't to be revered, because of course it is. The Bible says, "Neither is there salvation in any other: for there is none other name under heaven given among men, whereby we must be saved," (Acts 4:12). But we are not saved simply by knowing the name of Jesus. We are saved by trusting in Jesus' sufficient sacrifice to pay for our sins. By placing our faith in Him as the Son of God, we become sons of God.

The truth is that there are many churches throughout Latin America where the name of Jesus is mentioned, but sadly the gospel is nowhere to be found. This state of confusion only obscures the true message of salvation. The closer a lie is to the truth, the more dangerous it becomes. In other words, when someone hears that a church has something to do with Jesus (i.e. the Church of Jesus Christ of Latter-Day Saints), they think this church offers a Christian message. But this is far from the truth. No one goes to a Buddhist Temple to learn about Jesus, but many may go to a church seeking the truth, only to be given a version of Jesus that is a lie.

The need in Latin America is the same as the need in all of the world: gospel-centered churches that preach and teach what the Bible says. Without the gospel, those in Latin America are without hope!

The Bible says in 1 Corinthians 15:34, "Awake to righteousness, and sin not; for some have not the knowledge of God: I speak this to your shame." It is our responsibility to spread the gospel around the world. There are well over one million people in a seven-kilometer radius from our church in Buenos Aires, Argentina. Most of them would quickly say they "know" who God is, but that they have never accepted Jesus as Savior. Jesus said in John 14:6, "I am the way, the truth, and the life: no man cometh unto the Father, but by me." So it is impossible to know God without having accepted Jesus as Savior. These two truths, that it is our responsibility to bring people to a relationship with God and that it is impossible to know God without accepting Jesus, determine the need for church-planting missionaries in Latin America.

All of this may sound great, but even better are specific examples of people whose lives were transformed after hearing the gospel for the first time.

Matias had attended our church for over a year. He was never faithful, but when he came, he seemed happy to be there. Matias had cancer two years ago and had surgery to remove the tumor, but the fear of dying remained in the back of his mind. A few months ago, these fears increased. After a service one night, I asked him where he would go if he were to die. He told me he knew he wasn't saved. He told me he had listened to the gospel in our church, knew he needed to be saved, but had never placed his faith in Jesus. Matias believed on Jesus a few days later. He said he had never heard the gospel until he visited our church!

Amanda started attending our church because of a friend. She comes with her six-year-old daughter. Amanda's last name is Muhammad. Her grandparents were Muslim immigrants from the Middle East, but her parents adopted the Catholic faith because of its influence here in Argentina. Amanda had never heard the gospel, even though she attended Mass and graduated from a Catholic school. I remember the afternoon she was saved. When we asked about her salvation, she said she thought she was saved because she took of the Eucharist (The Catholic version of the Lord's supper in which they believe the elements become the literal body and blood of Jesus). After we explained the gospel to her, she accepted Jesus as her Savior and was baptized shortly thereafter.

Siblings Janet and Antonio started coming due to English classes we were offering. Their parents also started attending church with them. They are Peruvians who moved to Argentina over 10 years ago, and during one of the services, they heard the gospel. Janet came to me afterward and asked what I was talking about when I said we are sinners and needed to be saved. We talked for a moment, and she and her brother left, not quite understanding everything. They invited us over to their home to celebrate her son's birthday, and after dinner, Janet asked me to explain the gospel to them. We went through what the Bible said, and all four received Jesus as their Savior! Although they had heard the name of Jesus since birth, they had never heard the gospel.

Ricardo started coming to the church a few months ago. He came from a broken family, and the results of sin had taken a toll on his life, leaving him empty and dissatisfied. As we sat down in the church office, I began to explain the gospel to him. He seemed confused by it all. Like most people, he thought going to church meant he was a Christian, and that going to heaven depended on how he lived and whether the good things he had done outnumbered the bad things. After a long conversation, he told me he would think about what I said. He had never truly heard the gospel before, in a country in which Jesus is a common name!

In Mexico, the story is much the same.

Alfredo was a man who had drinking, anger, and marital problems. Today, he is a sweet, kind-hearted man who is leading his family biblically and prays some of the most precious prayers that I (Jonathan) have ever heard! Let me tell you his story.

Alfredo was just like most people without Christ. He and his wife had so many problems in their marriage and family that they had given up on resolving them. They were just going to act as if everything were okay. His wife had no respect for him, and he had relinquished any hope of having a good marriage.

Alfredo's family sent him to a Catholic retreat hoping he could get help and change his life. He stayed the necessary time, and they even had a welcome home party for him when he returned. The idea was that he was now a changed man! He could now finally be the man that his wife always wanted, and his children would now look up to him.

Far from the end of the story, Alfredo's home life only grew more frustrating. He ended up going back to the same habits. He began to drink, the anger returned, and he was once again frustrated and without hope of ever becoming the man that God and his family had hoped he would be.

Alfredo grew up hearing the name of Jesus. He knew that Jesus died on the cross for his sins. In his mind, Jesus was a good man. So why then was he not able to change? Because knowing facts about Jesus doesn't change lives. Only knowing Jesus Himself does.

Contrary to popular belief, the gospel is not readily available in Mexico. There are many churches that preach and teach what man can do in order to find God's favor. What is not preached is that Jesus did what man cannot do for himself. He died in his place and paid the price that only God in the flesh could pay.

A person can attend church, get baptized, or try to be a kind person toward others. He can give and even pray to a god without ever knowing the one true God. None of this will take him to heaven if his faith and trust is not solely in Jesus and His finished work on the cross.

In June 2014, Alfredo realized for the first time that solely knowing about Jesus was not enough. He realized that he could indeed know Him as his personal Savior. Alfredo decided to come to our first church service at Iglesia Bautista Nueva Vida (New Life Baptist Church) with his wife. What they heard that Sunday forever changed their lives. That day, he was able to understand the true gospel for the first time.

Most of Mexico and Latin America still need to hear what Alfredo heard that day. Approximately 85% of Latin Americans still believe in good works as the way to enter heaven. In fact, Alfredo had already lived over 60 years of his life before hearing the gospel!

One Sunday morning after he was saved, I asked Alfredo to pray for the service, thinking that he could probably do it. He looked at me with fear in his eyes and said in front of the whole church, "I don't know what to say, Pastor." I encouraged him to just thank God for the service, but he was completely frozen and could only get a few words out before looking at me with fear again. This was a man who knew how to rehearse prayers in the Catholic Church, but had just been saved and was nervous about praying in public.

Sometime later, we were invited to celebrate Alfredo's birthday with him and his family. I was wondering if he would want me to pray as his pastor and how he would handle the situation. As the time drew closer to pray for the food, his wife looked more anxious with every second that passed. She finally looked at him as if to say, "Who is going to bless the food, honey?" At that moment, Alfredo closed his eyes and started to thank God for his family and how blessed he was to have us with him in his home. Just when we all thought his prayer was over, he said these words: "God, I am so happy!"

How could this happen? Through the preaching of God's Word! God has truly changed and is continuing to change Alfredo's life.

Sadly, the story of Alfredo is not the story of most people in Latin America. There are thousands of graves in the cemetery just minutes from our churches in Mexico. They are full of people who could have been rescued from the flames of hell, but weren't. Perhaps if somebody had come to tell them that hearing or simply knowing the name of Jesus is not enough, they too could have been saved.

Diego is Alfredo's son-in-law. He knew so much about Catholicism and had heard the name of Jesus his whole life. Both of his parents serve as deacons in the Catholic Church and speak of Jesus on a daily basis in the home. Yet with all that his parents could offer, this was not enough for Diego to see and understand his need for the Savior. It was after he came to our church on a Sunday morning in December 2014, that God used the Bible and preaching to show him what true salvation is. A few days later in our living room, my Bible open in front of him, Diego accepted Jesus as his Savior.

One day, Alfredo's granddaughter came out of her room with a box in her hands. She looked at her mom and said, "I do not need these things anymore." The box that she had removed from her room was full of different saints, the Virgin Mary, and some holy water that she got from her extended family. She grew up thinking that Jesus was a good person, and she always had an image in her head of Jesus on the cross. She knew about Him. She was so close to the truth, and yet so far away. She gave the box to her mom that day and said, "Mom, I don't need these things anymore. I have Jesus, Who died for me, and He is enough."

Before all was said and done, we saw eight people get saved from that family! God changed four generations because we were able to get there in time with the gospel.

There are many more stories that can be recounted of others who have attended or are attending our churches, but there is a common link in Latin America: the vast majority of people have never heard the true gospel of Christ and therefore are not saved.

Could it be that God is wanting to use your life to reach people like Alfredo, Matias, and Amanda? Do you realize that we must go and tell them the good news? If these stories don't move you, could it be that you have a cold heart toward the need in this world?

God is working in Latin America. People are putting their faith in Jesus, but as He said, "The harvest truly is plenteous, but the labourers are few; Pray ye therefore the Lord of the harvest, that he will send forth labourers into his harvest," (Matthew 9:37). God is searching for laborers. Why couldn't one of them be you?

What Led Me To Latin America

Blake Young

"South America is already reached with the gospel."

If you think that, then come and see Medellin, Colombia.

Because what I saw there broke my heart.

I grew up in a home where I was told my mom did not love me and that my grandparents stole me away from her. I didn't even meet my dad for several years. I grew up angry and bitter, with so much hatred in my heart. Then I learned that God loved me and had taken an interest in my life. When God saved me, I learned "that he died for all, that they which live should not henceforth live unto themselves, but unto him which died for them, and rose again," (1 Corinthians 5:15). For the first time in my life, I realized I had a purpose, and that purpose was to live for Christ.

A few years later, I had an opportunity to visit several countries in the United Kingdom. It was there that God showed me that there was a need for the gospel all over the world. Later, I went to Nepal. I knew at the end of that trip that God had called me to missions, but I had no idea where He was leading me to serve.

Then, a seemingly random opportunity arose for me to go to Colombia. Upon arriving, I saw a country with beautiful mountains, friendly people, and awesome food. But what I saw a few days into that trip changed my life. Missionary Miguel Sanabria took my friends and me to a Catholic school where they worshipped the saint Mother Laura. I saw several school children praying to her in unison, and I heard their teacher tell them that if they wanted Mother Laura to bless their family and take them to heaven, that they needed to obey their teachers and parents. I saw a small room with three walls covered in about 800 plaques dedicated to Mother Laura, saying, "Thank you for providing for my family," "Thank you for giving me a job," and, "Thank you for healing my sick daughter."

After that day, as beautiful and friendly as Colombia was, my eyes were opened to the hurting masses around me. And that's why we're going to Colombia. We are going because there are so many who are just like I was, who will never hear the truth because they are blinded by religion. I met people who grew up the way I did, Colombians who believe that God has forsaken them, that they should have never been born, and that God is too busy for them. I saw hurting and angry families at a cemetery weeping over the death of their loved ones. They so strongly believe that if someone prays over their dead family member for 72 hours straight, that person can go to heaven.

What if we changed the way we think about Latin America? They are not reached with the gospel, yet God is doing something absolutely amazing there in our lifetime. There have been tens of thousands who have left the Catholic Church over the years, but there are so few churches preaching the truth, that they are finding churches that continue to preach a false work-based religion. They desperately need to hear the true gospel of Christ.

What do you think? Are they reached, or do you need to go and tell them about Christ?

CHAPTER 5

Self Versus Servant

*What if you lived for what God created
you to do?*

<u>*Kason Bloom*</u>

On January 8, 1956, five men were waiting on a river beach in the jungles of Ecuador. They were not there to have a good time. They were not there to look for oil or other natural resources. They were there because they knew close by were some of the world's most savage tribes, the Auca Indians. These Indians had a reputation for being adept with a spear and killing anyone who came near them. These five men knew this, but they were there anyway. They were there because they wanted to share the gospel with this tribe. They knew that there was a chance they might get killed, but this did not deter them in any way. Long ago, they had made up their minds that serving Jesus was more important than anything else in this world, including their own lives.

As you probably know, the Auca Indians did come out with their spears and kill those five missionaries. This attack made national news, and people all around the world heard about it. Many other young men surrendered to go to the mission field to take their place, and the deaths of these five missionaries provided an opening for others to take the gospel to this tribe.

Although it can be argued that they didn't make the smartest tactical move, I do believe that God greatly used them. Also, I think that they had the right attitude going into the situation. I have read several of their journals and have been struck by their singular desire to serve and live for Jesus.

Jim Elliot wrote in his journal:

"I seek not a long life, but a full one, like you, Lord Jesus."
"When it comes time to die, make sure that all you have to do is die."
"If we are the sheep of His pasture, remember that sheep are headed for the altar."

Nate Saint said, "I would rather die now than to live a life of oblivious ease in so sick a world." He also wrote, "People who do not know the Lord ask why in the world we waste our lives as missionaries. They forget that they too are expending their lives...and when the bubble has burst they will have nothing of eternal significance to show for the years they have wasted."

One thing I can tell you is that these men had a desire to live or die for Christ! It is a stark contrast to what I see in the world today. The world we live in today is a world that tells us to live for ourselves. It tells us to follow our hearts and our dreams. We must look inside ourselves to find happiness. It is a world that tells us it is okay to sin as long as we are doing it to help ourselves. We live in a world where we post pictures to social media and everyone gives us "likes" and "hearts" so we can feel good. It is the world of Instagram and Facebook. We judge our self-worth based upon how many "likes" we get or what others say about us. We live in a world that tells us to live for ourselves, but I would like to challenge you to serve Jesus and stop living for yourself.

Some of you might be thinking to yourselves right now that I am not talking to you because you are a Christian and aren't living for the things of this world. You are going to church, and you are serving in your church. That is wonderful, but I would like to remind you that it is possible to go to church and still be living for yourself, perhaps without even realizing it.

I have had the wonderful opportunity to travel around America to raise support as a missionary. It was a great time, and I was able to meet many wonderful Christians. I am thankful for all the churches that are supporting missions. As I traveled, I would meet many young men, and I always enjoyed talking to them about what they wanted to do with their lives. It was very sad to me that almost every single time I spoke to a young man, he had no plans to serve the Lord full-time or go to the foreign field as a missionary. Most of them were more worried about getting a job or getting a girlfriend. They wanted to join the army or work in construction. While there is nothing wrong with any of those things, I did think it was disappointing that almost nobody that I talked to said that they wanted to do something for God or that they wanted to serve Him with their lives.

I hope that reading this book will encourage you to live for the Lord, and in this chapter, I would like to share with you three reasons why you should serve Jesus and not live for self.

Living for Self Does not Produce Eternal Rewards

I remember the first time I learned about the word "million." For some reason I can't explain, that word intrigued me. A thousand thousands. Until that point in my life, I only knew numbers up to a thousand. While a thousand seemed like a significant number, a million just blew my mind. I could not fathom it. I remember playing a game called "Auction" with my siblings, and everyone would be bidding until I said a million. I knew I was always going to win with that big of a number. I remember telling my parents that I loved them "a million" because I knew that was a vast, unfathomable amount. To me, at that age, a million was bigger and longer than I could have ever imagined.

Of course, you are probably thinking to yourself that I was pretty stupid. Everybody knows that there are many more numbers than a million. There is a billion, and there is a trillion, and there are numbers to the 80th power. However, I want you to think for a moment about how long a million years would be. What would you do for a million years? What is possible to accomplish over a million years? How would it feel to live that long? The truth is that every person will know. The Bible tells us that there is life after death and that we will go to one of two places: heaven or hell. I am assuming that if you are reading this, you are a Christian and on your way to heaven. However, I want to ask you about the people who don't know about Jesus. What about that young boy in Peru? Or that old lady in Ecuador? Or that teenage girl in Chile? What are their first million years going to look like? What are they going to feel? What are they going to think? After that first million years, what about the millions upon billions upon trillions of years after that?

The reason I want you to consider this is that when you start to think about others, you stop living for yourself. I want you to consider what you should be living for in light of eternity. Does the career or plan that you have for your life consider the fact that we only have a short time on this earth? Does it account for the reality that our earthly lives are just a speck in eternity? I am writing this right now assuming that you are living for yourself and your plans. The reason I think this is because people are selfish. I know that I am selfish, and I know that pretty much every human being on this planet is selfish. We live for ourselves and make plans for ourselves. Almost everything that we do is for our own benefit. However, as Christians, the Bible says that we should no longer live for ourselves, but for Jesus! "And that he died for all, that they which live should not henceforth live unto themselves, but unto him which died for them, and rose again," (2 Corinthians 5:15).

With this in mind, I would like to remind you that living for yourself does not bring eternal rewards. Yes, you might be able to make a lot of money, but in a million years, what good is that money going to be for you? You might become a famous athlete, but in a billion years, who is even going to know you? You might be able to live the American Dream, but in a trillion years, will you even remember it?

We must realize that only serving and living for Jesus brings eternal rewards. All this stuff on earth is temporary. It will burn up. It will pass away, and in a million years, none of it will matter. Jim Elliot said, "He is no fool who gives what he cannot keep to gain what he cannot lose." I want to tell you right now that, with eternity in view, it is unwise to live for yourself. If we believe the Bible, the logical decision is that we should stop living for ourselves and temporal things and start serving Jesus.

Serving Jesus is the Greatest Thing that You Could Do with Your Life

How much is a soul worth? Can we even put a price on a soul? Is there anything else in the world that is worth that much? If you give your life to serve Jesus full-time, then you are committing to working with souls. You are committing to working with the most valuable thing on this planet.

There are many wonderful professions, but one thing that makes a missionary different from any other profession is that a lost person can't be a missionary. At least, they can't be one that's proclaiming the truth. If you decided not to be a doctor, there wouldn't suddenly be a dearth of doctors in the world. If you were a missionary instead of a lawyer, people wouldn't find themselves without any legal representation. But if you decided you weren't going to be a missionary, there is at least the potential that somebody will not hear the gospel because of it. Being a missionary is perhaps the most distinct thing that you could do with your life that would be difficult to replace.

Please don't take this to mean that I think it is wrong if you or somebody you know works in any of the above jobs. I know many men of God who are doing these things, and I believe that God has used them greatly where they are. However, if you are a young man or woman, I would like to challenge you to consider what would be the most valuable thing that you would do with your life. You have your career ahead of you, and you are at the point of deciding what you are going to do for the next forty to fifty years. I would challenge you to look at it from an eternal point of view, and I would dare to say that from that standpoint, serving Jesus trumps everything!

Jesus Came to Serve

The best example that we have of service is the life of Jesus. Not only did He come to earth to live like us, but He came to serve. Think about what Jesus gave up to come to earth. He was the God of heaven. He was all-powerful and all-present. He created the world with His words. He created man from the dust of the earth. He had every right to stay in heaven and not do anything for us. But is that what He did? No! He came to this earth and limited Himself to become like us. He was the God of the universe, but gave up everything to die for us. He was willing to be mocked, cursed, and abused to save us from our sins. He was willing to go through the worst possible pain and suffering on the cross because He knew that there was a world that needed to be saved.

Jesus died to save us, but for some reason, we do not think that we are called to the same sacrificial life. We believe that we deserve a nice life. We deserve a comfortable life. We deserve to be happy and have everything we could ever want. Isn't it ironic how we are so glad that Jesus came to serve us and save us from our sins, but somehow we don't think that we should live like Him? We want to follow the American Dream. We want a nice house with a good-looking husband or wife and obedient kids, but we want to stay as far away as we can from being like Jesus! We don't want to take up our cross and follow Him. We are willing to go to church on Sunday morning, but we are not willing to give our lives entirely in service to Him.

Are you willing to give everything up to serve Jesus? Are you willing to become that living sacrifice? Romans 12:1 says, "I beseech you therefore, brethren, by the mercies of God, that ye present your bodies a living sacrifice, holy, acceptable unto God, which is your reasonable service." Are you willing to put Jesus first before everything else? Are you ready to put Him before your job, your friends, or your family? "If any man come to me, and hate not his father, and mother, and wife, and children, and brethren, and sisters, yea, and his own life also, he cannot be my disciple," (Luke 14:26).

Sometimes we think that living for ourselves means that we are living in sin and not going to church or reading our Bible. While this is true, I also believe that sometimes living for ourselves can mean that we are in church, and we are reading our Bible, but we are not concerned about the lost around us. We are thankful that we are saved, but we are not going to do anything to tell others. We are grateful that we have a good church, but we aren't concerned about the lives of the lost around the world. The Bible says in Matthew 9:37-38, "Then saith he unto his disciples, The harvest truly is plenteous, but the labourers are few; Pray ye therefore the Lord of the harvest, that he will send forth labourers into his harvest." We need to be like Jesus and be concerned about the need around the world. Perhaps God is calling you to be one of His servants in the harvest.

Are you living for yourself, or are you living for Jesus? If you are living for yourself, then something needs to change. Make the decision today that you are going to pattern your life after Christ, Who lived to serve others.

What Led Me To Latin America

Lauren Grant

"Awake to righteousness, and sin not; for some have not the knowledge of God: I speak this to your shame," (1 Corinthians 15:34).

Although I grew up in a Christian family and was saved at a young age, it was many years later that I first became exposed to missions. As the Lord began to give me a burden for missions, He started to show me the great need for the gospel that exists around this world, and I moved to Alpharetta, Georgia, to begin training for missions at the Our Generation Training Center in connection with Vision Baptist Church and Vision Baptist Missions. After a few months, I started to pray about where the Lord would have me go on a missions trip. God opened the door and provided the opportunity for me to visit the ministry in Arequipa, Peru.

It was during that trip that I knew that the Lord had not only called me into missions, but that He was calling me specifically to the country of Peru. Visiting the ministry in Peru opened my eyes and broke my heart for the great need that still exists among the people there!

I never imagined that I would be serving the Lord in full-time ministry, much less serving Him in another country. But the truth is that we, as Christians, need to awake to righteousness and sin not because there are people all around this world who do not have the knowledge of God. They do not have the truth of the gospel. There is a whole world out there that is lost and headed for hell! The situation is desperate, and we know of the Savior Who can give them the free gift of salvation. 1 Timothy 2:5 says, "For there is one God, and one mediator between God and men, the man Christ Jesus." And yet there are millions in Peru today who do not know that truth.

How can you look into the faces of men, women, boys, and girls who are striving so hard for their salvation and not desire to tell them the truth of the gospel? God gives us the command through His Word to go into all the world and tell others the truth. He gives us a desire in our hearts, and then He gives us an opportunity to serve Him. Latin America has a great need for the gospel, and there are millions of people who need to hear the truth! That command, that desire, and that need is what led me to Peru and Latin America.

CHAPTER 6

Scope

What if you saw the vast opportunities in Latin America?

Stephen Underwood

Three days, two countries, one rainy night on a park bench, and one bed in a hostel with three other guys... This was how I finally made it to Tucuman, Argentina! The trip was eye-opening and heart-wrenching. As we crossed over the Andes Mountains through the Peruvian countryside into Bolivia, there was one common thread that I simply couldn't escape: people had very little hope.

The toil life had taken on each of them was evident. I saw how they loved their families, raised their children, worked to provide and meet their needs, all the while having no hope of anything better in this life or the next.

And my heart broke.

I asked God to allow me to come back one day and share with them the greatest news they could ever hear. I asked Him to allow me to be His messenger of hope to a hopeless people. I asked Him to allow me the opportunity to be a part of His plan to reach the world, which includes Latin America, with the gospel of Jesus Christ.

As I look back on that experience, and I think about how my calling to the mission field came to be, I can't help but be reminded of Paul's experience in Acts 17. He was in the city of Athens and saw among all the superstition an altar dedicated to "The Unknown God." The Bible says his heart was stirred within him. One thing that's obvious is that the apostle Paul knew an opportunity when he saw one. In this situation, he didn't merely pass by with a glance, but instead took advantage of the situation. *Why*, he must have thought, *here is an opportunity to declare Jesus Christ to these people. The situation is perfect.*

With great boldness, Paul stood and declared the gospel to those Athenians on Mars Hill. And, contrary to what many might have thought would happen, some of them believed. In fact, at least one of those who believed bore the name of a false Greek god! But what if Paul had stared at that altar, noticed the opportunity, and done nothing about it? Or what if he had been so consumed with his own thoughts that he didn't even see the possibility that lay right in front of him?

One need only to look at the book of Esther to see another example of a person's seeing an opportunity and taking advantage of it. After the Jews had been sentenced to death by the king due to Haman's trickery, Mordecai wasted no time in seeing how God had worked things out to save them. He sent word to Esther that she would have to speak out in defense of her people, and in what is perhaps one of the most recognizable Bible quotes, he asks her, "Who knoweth whether thou art come to the kingdom *for such a time as this?*" While he couldn't be completely sure, Mordecai had a good idea that Esther was meant to be the one to save her people from Haman's massacre. He looked at the situation and realized there was somebody in a position to do something. To her credit, instead of panicking and depending on somebody else to do the job, Esther saw her responsibility in the matter and took the risk.

Sometimes an opportunity is so great that a person can't possibly pass it up. This was the case with Paul and Esther. But what about you?

Could it be that God has been preparing Latin America *for such a time as this?* Could it be that He knew you'd be born at the time you were and that He would have you ready to go there? Could it be that there is a young person in Paraguay, Uruguay, Brazil, or some other Latin American country that God wants to reach through you, and He has brought you both into this world at the same time for that purpose?

What might Paul say to us now? Perhaps he would say, "You have an opportunity to do something to reach this world with the gospel. Why are you sitting around doing nothing? Look at Latin America, and how God has opened the door there! Go take advantage of it!"

What about Esther? She might say, "No matter what it may cost you, take that step of faith. I stepped out to save my people from a physical death. You must decide that you will step out to deliver others from Satan's grasp. And if you perish, you perish. But, like me, you will have done what you were meant to do."

There have been great movements of God throughout the centuries in certain times and in certain places. Just read about the Great Awakening in America, and how God used that time in American colonial history to shape what is so much of modern-day America. At least one of us writing in these pages comes from a church that was started out of one of those revivals. Why? Because God was moving, and preachers of the gospel took the opportunity He had handed them.

We believe Latin America may be on the cusp of its own Great Awakening, but as the Holy Spirit is moving, are we ready to allow Him to work through us? Or will we let the opportunity pass by? Will we always wonder what could have been?

We could have seen a great moving of the Lord, had there been men and women willing to respond to His call.

Latin America could have been reached in such a great way with the gospel, but...

Or, worst of all: *God wanted to do something, but we limited Him,* (Psalm 78:41).

A man once said, "We must plant seed where it's raining." God is doing something incredible in Latin America. The scales of religion are beginning to fall from people's eyes as they see the abuses in the Catholic Church and turn from religious tradition. People are hungry for the truth, if only someone will give it to them.

And that is where we have an incredible opportunity of which we must take advantage. As of this writing, nearly every single country in Latin America is open and has religious freedom. A person can go just about anywhere, announce that they are there as a missionary, and be allowed in with the same rights and access as anybody else. There are several churches in Latin America due to the great open door God has placed there, but the work remains unfinished. There is still so much more to be done.

Statistics may be vital in understanding the numbers alone, but what will really make a difference in your heart is turning those statistics into faces, names, and souls. What will really make a difference is knowing that those souls will face eternity. Until you see that, there is no amount of enticing words I can write that would move you to forsake your own dreams and follow God's. I truly believe the reason that more do not surrender to take the gospel to the foreign field is because we have trained ourselves to disconnect what we see from the reality of eternity.

If we are truly to have a burden for Latin America, then simply knowing the need isn't enough. We must awake to understand that they have an eternal soul! That eternal soul will one day face judgment. We must remember that those who die lost without Christ will forever be separated from Him and tormented in hell.

What if you saw the vast opportunities in Latin America? What if you saw the 15 million souls in Buenos Aires? The millions in Santiago? La Paz? Mexico City? Would it move you to lay aside your excuses, desires, and goals? Would you instead find the most rewarding and fulfilling purpose this world has ever seen? Would you declare, with an uplifted hand and an open heart, as the Prophet Isaiah did, "Lord, here am I, send me!"

What Led Me To Latin America

Andrew Garcia

I was seven years old when I asked God to save me from my sins. I placed my faith in Him and in His finished work on the cross. I was saved by faith alone and not by any work or merit. Christ did all the work for me. Soon after that, I told my pastor I wanted to be a missionary; but after my parents' divorce, I lost interest in serving God. However, when I was 15, I surrendered my life to do whatever God called me to do.

I graduated from Pensacola Christian College with a degree in missions in 2016. Before and even after graduating, I was set on being a missionary to Japan. I started learning Japanese and studying the culture. There is certainly a great need there. After I graduated, I went to Honduras as part of a mission team with Pensacola Christian College. From there, God led me to agree to stay in Honduras and teach in a Christian school for two years. I figured it would be a good experience. During my time there, God drew my attention to the need for missions in Honduras. I also came to the realization that Honduras, like all of Latin America, has the potential to be a great sender of missionaries. There is no reason at all that God can not greatly use Latin Americans to take the gospel to the uttermost.

From 2016 to 2018, I was a teacher at a bilingual Christian school in Honduras. I got to teach Bible to my students every morning and had some opportunities to preach in chapel. I went out on evangelism weekly and was part of a bus route to pick up people to bring to church. I learned a lot of Spanish while I was there.

I could tell you about the poverty in Honduras. I could tell you about the fatherless children. I could talk to you about the crime. But today I'm here to talk to you about the lost souls of Honduras. Honduras is home to over ten million people, and while Catholicism is a little less common than it used to be, the majority of Hondurans still believe that they must do good to go to heaven. They do not know the gospel message of Ephesians 2:8-9, which says, "For by grace are ye saved through faith; and that not of yourselves: it is the gift of God: Not of works, lest any man should boast."

I pray that God will quickly send me to the field so that I may win souls for Christ and start churches in the capital, Tegucigalpa. My main goal will be to make disciples, training men of God for the ministry. I long to see pastors who will carry the gospel throughout the country of Honduras, and God willing, throughout the entire world.

CHAPTER 7

Strength

What if you focused on Jesus' strength instead of your weakness?

<u>Wayne Cooke</u>

"For I am not ashamed of the gospel of Christ: for it is the power of God..." (Romans 1:16).

Relying on God's Strength in our Preparation

Growing up in the country, especially in the South, we boys were always trying to prove our strength. We wanted to know who could throw a rock the furthest, climb the tallest tree, run the fastest, etc. This is not to mention all the sports in which we were involved.

As I grew up, I was always the shortest guy in my class until about the 5th grade. This bothered me and made me try even harder to impress those around me. I was always trying to prove that I could do it, whatever the "it" was. In high school, I tried out for the wrestling team and made varsity my first year. I was so proud because I had accomplished something.

But the notion of relying on my own strength changed my junior year during the commissioning service of a missionary on his way to Brazil, South America. God began to touch my heart about serving Him in the area of foreign missions. I immediately became afraid and started giving Him excuses: *Not me, I can't speak well, I'm shy, I'm timid, I'm backwards.* All of my so-called talents were quickly forgotten in light of the seriousness of the call being placed on my life. Whereas I wasn't scared before to try new things and be adventurous, I knew that I alone couldn't do what was now being asked of me. I needed help. I needed Him!

After arguing with the Lord the entire service, I finally surrendered during the invitation to go wherever it was that He wanted. The next few years were filled with both excitement and difficulty. Finishing high school, starting Bible college, getting married, and then graduating from Bible college-all of these were wonderful, yet trying times. My wife and I relied on the Lord heavily during this time of preparation.

We weren't alone in this. In the Bible, King David passed through several situations in which he needed God's strength before he finally ascended the throne. He killed a lion and a bear while watching his father's sheep, and upon seeing the giant Goliath, he recalled these experiences. His killing Goliath was something the Lord used to catapult him into a prominent position among the people, but it wasn't long before his life was in danger again, this time from the hand of Saul. During his years as a fugitive, he relied heavily on the Lord's strength. Yet all of this was preparing him for the years to come. He could have done none of this, had not the Lord been his Helper.

For Our Power

The next phases of deputation and language school proved once again that we needed Him and Him alone to finish the task. After starting the first church in Villa Hermosa, Guatemala, we watched God bring people and change lives by His power and through His gospel. Many times, we would mess up in the language or culturally offend someone and would have to apologize for our wrong. Yet God would turn it into something wonderful!

I remember once I was preaching in Honduras for a friend. Upon arriving in his city, we went to eat supper. During the conversation that evening, he bragged on how well I spoke Spanish. Boy, was that a mistake! I could immediately feel my head swelling with pride, but God has a way of deflating us. Surely enough, the sound system went out during one of the first services, and I had to practically yell the rest of the week. The last night of revival, I was tired and discouraged because no one was getting saved. I actually said, "I don't know what else I could do or say," and it was as if God had been waiting for me to step out of the way all along. That night, seventeen people came forward to make professions of faith! Many times, all God wants is for us to stop trying to do His work in our strength alone and to start relying on Him. That is when things will happen. God is looking for men who will not only follow Him, but fall on Him and trust in His strength for power.

For Our Protection

Not only do we need to trust Him for our preparation and for power in the work, but also for protection. While writing this, my family and I were out doing some shopping near our home. While we were at the little mall, my wife was inside one of the stores buying groceries, and my daughter and I were outside in an open-air food court drinking a Coke. Everything was fine until, all of a sudden, about thirty yards from where we were sitting, a motorcycle pulled up with two men on it. The man on the back of the motorcycle began to open fire with his pistol, shooting into the bus that was waiting there for passengers. One bullet struck the driver in the chest, but no one else was hit. God was protecting us from stray bullets and allowing us to not be in the line of fire. I could tell you countless other stories when only God was the answer to our escape from a bad situation.

God's strength always supersedes man's strength. Think of Shadrach, Meshach, and Abednego. The wicked King Nebuchadnezzar declared that they would bow to his graven image or die in the fiery furnace. Upon declaring that they would never worship anything but the one true God, they were condemned to die. Yet when the king looked into the furnace, He saw the Son of God walking in the fire along with them. He discovered moreover that not even the hairs of their heads were singed! Those flames were no match for God.

When you surrender to go to the mission field, you will go through fires. But you will always find that God is with you in them. And His strength is greater than that of any man's.

To Fulfill His Purpose

We need God's strength to fulfill His purpose. God only uses those who are weak in His presence. In 1 Corinthians 1:26-29, we find whom God chooses and whom He uses. We do not find Him choosing the wise, mighty, or noble. We do, however, find Him going after the foolish, weak, and base things. He uses things which are not, the nothings and nobodies.

One nobody that God used to fulfill His purpose is found in the book of Judges. The children of Israel had once again sinned against God, and he had delivered them into the hands of the Midianites. These godless enemies oppressed them mightily, and Israel cried out to God for deliverance. The Bible says, "And there came an angel of the Lord, and sat under an oak which was in Ophrah, that pertained unto Joash the Abiezrite: and his son Gideon threshed wheat by the winepress, to hide it from the Midianites. And the angel of the Lord appeared unto him, and said unto him, The Lord is with thee, thou mighty man of valour."

Gideon asked why all this evil had happened to them if the Lord was really with them, and the response was that he, Gideon, would be the one to deliver Israel from the Midianites. Gideon could hardly believe his ears. "Oh my Lord," he said, "wherewith shall I save Israel? behold, my family is poor in Manasseh, and I am the least in my father's house."

Gideon looked at himself at that moment and saw only his own weakness. God, however, saw what Gideon could accomplish in the strength of the Lord. And, true to His word, Gideon did deliver the Israelites.

Maybe you want to be a missionary, but you're not sure you have the strength to do it. You know your weaknesses, and in your mind, those are too much to overcome. And you're right. In your own strength, they are. But in God's strength, you too can be like Gideon. Perhaps you are just the person God is looking for to bring light to those who are lost in Latin America.

Why would an almighty, all-knowing, all-present God choose to operate this way? "That no flesh should glory in His presence," (1 Corinthians 1:29). I think we would all agree that our Heavenly Father knows best. So let it be a great consolation and sweet comfort seeing His purpose not only in our individual lives, but also in the entire world. He wants and deserves all of the glory! Let's embrace the wonderful truth of relying on Him and His strength! You don't have to be the smartest, best-looking, most-talented, or most-educated person for God to use you in Latin America. So lay aside those fears, because His strength is made perfect in your weakness.

What Led Me To Latin America

Andrew Wilder

To be honest, in regards to how God led me to Latin America, I didn't have this lightning bolt hit me, nor did I have this strange feeling that I should go to Bolivia as a missionary. Rather, I saw it as an opportunity to serve the Lord in a needy place. If we take the Bible literally, then we know that there is a world out there that is dying and going to hell. And it is up to us to go into all the world and tell people about Jesus. Of course, there is a need here in the States, but there is a much greater need outside of the U.S.

Latin America is definitely one of those needy places. In Bolivia, where God has called me, more missionaries are needed. There are over 11 million people in the country and very few missionaries trying to reach those 11 million people. That is why I must go to Bolivia and share the gospel of Jesus Christ with them.

For some reason, God has always put Latin American people in my life. My best friend in middle school and high school was Hispanic. I feel like God was preparing me even back then to work with people in Latin America. I remember sitting with Hispanics at lunch and playing soccer with them as well. God has always given me a heart for people, and He led me to Latin America. Ultimately, it was God all along directing my path. I never thought I would be a missionary, but God had bigger plans than I could ever imagine.

I got saved at the age of seven, but when I was in high school, all I wanted to do was play sports. During my senior year, I remember asking myself, "What am I going to do with my life?" This is when I began to question God's will for my life and wondered what the next step was. I later decided to go to Reinhardt University, although I went with all the wrong motives. I went to play football. While playing in a football game one day, I got injured. I tore the labrum in my shoulder, and that meant that I had to have surgery. The surgery took place during my college Christmas break, and while recovering, I was back at my parents' house attending my home church.

During a service, I met a missionary by the name of Brendon Wung. He was there presenting his ministry, and after the service, he spoke to my brother and me about the Our Generation Camp. At the time, I thought it would be just like any other camp, but little did I know that it would change my life forever.

After recovering from surgery and returning for my second semester of college, I continued to seek God's will for my life. I attended a great Baptist church that encouraged me to live my life for God, and it was during this second semester *that I finally decided to do something for God. I decided to live my life for Him and not just for myself. This led to my withdrawing from Reinhardt University, as I was still considering God's will for my life. I then began the process of joining the National Guard because I thought this was what God wanted me to do.*

Around that time, the Our Generation Camp took place. This is a camp hosted by Vision Baptist Church and Vision Baptist Missions that is all about missions and the need for the gospel around the world. While at the camp, I realized that it was not God's plan for me to join the military, but my plan alone. I had been blinded by what I wanted to do long enough and finally saw that God had been calling me to serve Him as a missionary.

I went to get training for missions at the Our Generation Training Center for three years, and afterwards spent six months in Bolivia as a missionary intern with veteran missionary Kevin White. During my internship, God burdened my heart for the lost people of Bolivia, and I am now on my way back as a church-planting missionary!

CHAPTER 8

Strategy

What if you followed Christ's method for missions?

Jason Holt

My expectations were high my freshman year at Bible college as I entered the first class of the *Introduction to Missions* course. My heart was thrilled to finally hear a biblical strategy of how we could reach the world with the gospel in our generation. *Finally*, I thought, *I'm going to learn what a missionary is and does, and how I can become one.*

Just a couple of weeks before the start of classes, I had returned from my first missions trip. It was originally a weeklong trip that turned into a month's stay, but that's another story for another day. Coming off that pivotal trip to Mexico, my heart burned to know how my life could impact the scattered cities and communities of Latin America. For the first time, I had seen huge, largely-populated areas with no access to a Bible-preaching church. My heart was heavy and my mind was eager to devour anything on the subject of world evangelization.

But despite all the lectures and required reading in my course, I struggled to solidify a clear biblical strategy in my mind. I thought, *If reaching the world with the gospel was the main task Jesus gave His church, surely there must be a clear way to accomplish it. He didn't command us to do something impossible, did He?* But instead of walking away from that course with all the training and tools to engage the Great Commission, I walked away understanding clearly that **the modern missions movement has utterly failed**. Traditional mission methods (as defined by the recent decades) weren't even keeping pace with the population growth. Each day, we were further from the goal than the previous day. We were losing ground.

Were we destined to never reach the world with the gospel? Was it even possible? Is God making an unrealistic demand of us? Did He tell us to go to the world while knowing that it was impossible? I was a confused and frustrated eighteen-year-old, but I was determined to search for a path forward.

A few things did become clear after that *Intro. to Missions* class. The traditional missions method would never reach the world with the gospel. For decades, missionaries had spent one term (four years) planting one church. Their goal during that time was to train and leave one national pastor behind to lead the young church. There are some obvious weaknesses with this method. For one, it is difficult to leave a mature church in four years, much less to see a man saved, discipled, and trained in that time frame. Following this traditional pattern, a forty-year missions career would only produce eight infant church plants that struggle to remain faithful in doctrine and practice over time. And, let's be honest, there are very few missionaries who spend forty years or more on the field! Eight churches in forty years, which is the best-case scenario, isn't going to accomplish the goal of world evangelization. **This is our dilemma. The world is growing at astronomical speeds, and our traditional method struggles to make a meaningful difference.**

What if we traded our traditional methods for biblical ones? What if there were a way to see the world evangelized? What if the Great Commission were a command we could fulfill in our generation? Well, prepare yourself. There is a way, and it's biblical!

Let's fast-forward a year past my *Intro. to Missions* course. As part of my college studies, I found myself living for six months in Peru, South America, with missionary Austin Gardner. I was studying "for the field, on the field," and I loved it! While there, I continued to grapple with these missiological issues, but I also started to see a methodology in Peru that might just be the answer for which I was looking.

The missions pattern I observed in Peru was based on these simple truths: train men for ministry, reproduce yourself, and make disciples.

While this shouldn't seem like an innovative approach, it was. The focus was not primarily on evangelism or church planting. It was on training men. Don't get me wrong. Evangelization and church planting was happening. But the ministry of men-training was the main objective.

Who else have we seen model this approach? Yes, you're right! It was Jesus. If you look at the methods Jesus used, they are the same. The vast majority of His time was spent with twelve men, teaching, mentoring, and preparing them to change the world. Mark 3:14 says, "And he ordained twelve, that they should <u>be with him</u>, and that he might <u>send them</u> forth to preach." Notice that He spent time with them, then He sent them. The relationship preceded the ministry. He trained men, and they changed the world.

This Jesus-like model was what I saw in action in Peru. The missionary spent lengthy amounts of time mentoring young men in their personal walk with the Lord, in their relationship with their spouses, and in their basic involvement in local church ministries. Then, as they grew in maturity, they were entrusted with deeper ministry and theological training. Although they did have formal classes, the mentor relationship was the key to it all. Soon many of these experienced men were being sent out of the local Peruvian churches to reach all of southern Peru with the gospel. What started with a small group of four or five men soon multiplied to over a hundred preparing for ministry. Each man reproduced himself through the same mentorship method. "Men training men" was the method Jesus used and the method I saw in practice while on my internship in Peru.

Soon, I noticed this method wasn't strictly Jesus' technique. Paul echoes a similar thought in 2 Timothy 2:2, "And the things that thou hast heard of me among many witnesses, the same commit thou to faithful men, who shall be able to teach others also." Paul taught Timothy. Timothy was then to teach faithful men. Those faithful men were enlisted to teach others. This is it! Training men who will train men is the key to reaching the world in our generation!

Think about it. Instead of starting one church every four years and then moving off to another city to start another church, what if we started a church and began to mentor as many young men as possible? What if we identified the faithful ones and entrusted them with greater responsibilities and opportunities? What if we could reproduce ourselves multiple times every year? Here's a little homework. Do the math based on a forty-year missions career. After the first year, there will be two disciples, because you reproduced yourself. At the end of the second year, the two multiplies to four, then eight, then sixteen, etc. You won't believe how much the number will grow over a forty-year span! Get your calculator because you will need it.

Let's fast-forward another five years past the internship in Peru. By then it was 2005, and I was twenty-four years old. My young family had already finished deputation and language school. We had settled into our new home in the metropolis of Santiago, Chile. It was time to plant our first church. I can't explain how excited I was at the prospect of seeing a church launched in a needy residential area of the city. By faith, we were ready to see this country changed by the gospel. As we searched street by street for a building to plant Faith Baptist Church (named appropriately because of the step of faith we were taking in this new and unfamiliar country), we asked God to lead us to where He would have us. And He did!

Fifty thousand people lived within a fifteen-minute walk of this little building! It's hard for some of us to imagine the population density of such a large city. There were literally tens of thousands of people to reach within a mile of the church. This was our Jerusalem, and we were eager to reach it with the gospel.

During the weeks leading up to the official inaugural service, we systematically canvassed ten thousand homes, five times each. We also started weekly evangelistic English classes. A recent Bible college graduate from Peru came to assist for a few months with all the work, and we ended up using two and three pairs of socks at a time to soften our blistered feet as we walked for dozens of hours each week. On a side note, I completely underestimated what it would take for the two of us to canvas ten thousand homes a week for five weeks in a row. Not to mention that I decided to double our efforts on the fifth week and hit twenty thousand homes!

We had 140 people show up to the first service. I was elated. We immediately transitioned to two Sunday morning services to accommodate the crowds. We didn't know exactly what God was doing, but we couldn't wait to find out!

The following week, about 95 people showed up to our Sunday morning services. The attendance dipped to about 70 the third week. Our fourth week brought a record low of 30, and that's where we leveled out. Most of those who came to our first service were curious neighbors who wanted to know who the new guy was in the neighborhood. Now their curiosity was satisfied, and they were back to their normal schedules on Sundays, schedules which didn't include attending Faith Baptist.

During this crazy first-church launch, Lori, my beautiful and incredibly supportive wife, was juggling ministry and motherly responsibilities. She was enjoying being a mother to our two-year-old daughter and four-month-old son – if you can call little sleep, constant crying, diaper changing, feeding, and cleaning "enjoyment." She was also taking on more and more responsibilities at the church plant. She would often play the piano while holding Josh, our four-month-old, in her lap. As soon as the music was over, she would rush off to the nursery to tend to our babies and the babies of the new converts who were growing slowly but surely. She also taught children's classes, discipled ladies, led special ladies' events, and made everything, and I mean *everything*, work more smoothly and efficiently. Everyone who knows us knows I'm the big-picture guy, and she's the nuts and bolts gal. I'm vision. She's details. Sometimes working together, we drive each other crazy, but we end up making a pretty awesome team!

As the first couple of months turned into the first couple of years, we saw God do some amazing things. Lives were gloriously changed by the gospel. Marriages were restored. The church grew to well over 100 in attendance. Sunday school teachers were being trained. Chileans were evangelizing and discipling Chileans. We were seeing sustained growth both numerically and spiritually. We ended many days exhausted but deeply satisfied by what God was doing through our little church in Santiago, Chile.

But there was a problem. Lori knew I had made a commitment that ended up dramatically extending our first term on the field. I decided from the beginning to not leave the church plant until a Chilean pastor was trained. I wouldn't turn the church over to another American missionary. We would continue serving until local leadership was able to lead. Training men was, after all, the biblical method to reach Chile and the world, right?

This initially clear understanding was quickly fogged by the relentless need to prepare weekly sermons, the ongoing hours of outreach, and the unending administration that this little church plant demanded. We were reaching people, but not training leaders. We were focused on the masses instead of the twelve. I was serving more as a pastor than a missionary, and I didn't even realize it.

Church growth had become the unspoken goal. The missiological conclusions from years before were lost amid the hustle and bustle of the church-planting grind. My head was down, and I was focused on the next visit, the next message, the next meeting. At this rate, we would never start another church. We would never take a furlough, for that matter!

Near the end of my second year at Faith Baptist, my missions mentor, Austin Gardner, came for a visit. I proudly took him to the church property that we had recently raised $120,000 to purchase. He preached to a packed house of growing young converts in this cramped mission-field church. I was proud of the church and proud of "my" people! But when we got home that night, he asked me a convicting question. "Where are your men?" For the next four or five days, I would hear him repeat that probing, yet simple question: "Where are the men you are training for ministry?"

He was right. Drawing a crowd was not the path to reaching Chile with the gospel. Building a large local church was great, but not the primary task of a missionary. I knew the answers but had lost myself in the process.

That week marked a turning point in the ministry. Many things changed in the weeks and months that followed. I spent more time mentoring the young men and began begging God to put the desire to preach in their hearts. We started a Bible institute, which was a prelude to today's Chile Training Center. My messages starting centering more on missions, surrender, service, and the book of Acts. God began to work.

During the next few months, three men from Faith Baptist surrendered their lives to the ministry. Before we took our first furlough (Six years and four months after arriving to Chile), we had three churches planted and a handful of young men trained for ministry. After several years of sputtering along, we began to work God's plan, and He gave the increase. God was saving Chilean souls. He was calling men to preach. It was God's work, and we were merely His servants. All praise be to our good God!

Through the team that God has brought together in Chile, we have now seen 10 churches planted, and we currently have over 50 young men and women preparing for local-church ministry at the Chile Training Center. With all the men who are preparing for church planting, the ministry in Chile could literally double in size during the next five years.

The process of following God's plan to train men reminds me of dominos. Do you remember as a child painstakingly standing each domino on its edge, one next to another? Did you ever crisscross the room with elaborate designs, only to see them all tumble once you pushed over the first one? That's the way missions works. Once you disciple and train that first church planter, he launches out to reproduce the process. Before you know it, he's training a few young guys who will soon be planting churches.

At the time of this writing in 2019, a young man named Josue is a few months away from planting his first church. He is being trained by Jorge. Jorge was reached and trained by Cristian, who was the first Chilean pastor I mentored back at Faith! That's a fourth-generation church planter! Soon Josue will undoubtedly be mentoring his first church-planting son in the faith. In the meantime, Cristian and Jorge will continue to train more and more young men for ministry. The multiplication process has started. The dominos are falling, and there's no way to stop it. Jesus is building His church. If I die today, the work will continue on in Chile because dozens of men have bought in to the biblical plan.

What we need now are men and women, full of faith, who will plunge into the depths of needy cities throughout Latin America with a passionate commitment to train men to plant churches, who will in turn train more men themselves. We need a few hundred who will give the next few decades of their lives to be that first domino to start something that will change an entire continent for God's glory.

Does it take time? Yes! It takes decades. The multiplication process is both grueling and glorious. Jesus spent three years preparing twelve men. They spent the rest of their lives reaching their generation with the gospel. It takes a lot of time to plant that first church. Sometimes you take two steps forward and three steps back. It takes a long time to see the multiplication of men and churches reach its full potential. A missionary hero of mine, Randy Stirewalt, said the key years in the multiplication process are between the 25th and 30th year of ministry. He observes that it's difficult to really make a significant difference in less time. By the way, Randy Stirewalt has seen over three hundred churches started with over seventy thousand in weekly attendance in Kenya. I've been there and seen it myself.

Is it easy? By no means. A small percentage of missionaries return to the field for their second or third terms. Most quit. Only by God's grace are we still on the field. And only by His grace will we continue to see many more trained like Cristian, Jorge, and Josue. But, with His help, we have put our hands to the plow, and we plan to be in Latin America for decades to come. There are too many fruitful fields still unplowed to consider leaving yet.

Can Latin America be reached in our generation? Of course! I know that's a bold response, but it's true. I left that freshman *Introduction to Missions* course doubting whether or not it was possible. But as I understood Jesus' and Paul's method, I understood that it is indeed still possible today. It's our desire that as you prayerfully read this book, you will join us and be a part of the multiplied force to reach Latin America.

Is it worth it? I can't even begin to explain the overwhelming, godly satisfaction of knowing your life has been wholly thrust, by faith, on the frontlines of Great Commission ministry. It's the greatest privilege you could imagine. We are living the dream. Literally.

Could you do this? Yes! We are talking about doing God's plan, His way, with His power. Our insecurities and fears reveal that we think we're the important pieces of the puzzle. We're not. He is. Lean in to Him by faith and obey His Great Commission.

What will you do? I'm not asking you for a couple of weeks on the field. I'm asking you to give your life to train men, plant churches, and see lives eternally changed by Jesus. I'm inviting you to one of the most fruitful and open areas in the world today – Latin America.

What Led Me To Latin America

Joshua Miller

I grew up in a Christian home. Memories of my youth are filled with believers investing in and sharing the gospel with me. Gospel witnesses surrounded me, yet I rejected this good news until I was 18 years old. At that time, the Holy Spirit convicted me of my sin and hypocrisy, and I received Christ as my Savior! Shortly after that, I went on my first missions trip to Peru, South America. I didn't know what to expect, but I was excited about my new life in Christ, and I wanted to see what was outside of the world in which I grew up.

I arrived in Peru and met David Gardner, the missionary with whom I would spend the next month. David invested in me and showed me how God could use my life to reach the world with the gospel. From my very first day in Peru, I started to realize that Peruvian culture and religious traditions were nothing like mine. I saw sincere people who were caught up in a system, trying to do anything they could to earn favor with God. They wanted so badly to be accepted by God, but they did not have the truth of God's Word. I considered my own testimony, how I rejected the gospel for so many years, and it astounded me that many of the Peruvians I saw would go their entire life without ever hearing the gospel.

The Lord used this experience to open my eyes to the need for the gospel around the world. All I knew was the situation I grew up in, but I did not consider that so many people around the world could live their whole life without the transforming message of God's Word! It took a trip to South America for God to show me how blessed I am and how He could use my life to be a blessing to others by sharing the gospel with them.

I want to encourage and challenge you to go on a missions trip. Visit a missionary with an established ministry and see what God is doing all over the world. You have been richly blessed, and there is no telling how God can use your life for His glory! Take the time and make the trip to see how God can burden your heart and use your life to reach others with the same gospel that reached you!

CHAPTER 9

Suppose

What if you were choosing a place to serve as a young person?

W. Austin Gardner

Several years ago, a good friend of mine who is now a missionary to Argentina, Shawn Bateman, came down to visit me in Alpharetta, Georgia. He was pastoring a church in South Carolina, and God was using him. He loved God, was hungry to serve God, and had a desire to do more that would have a larger, more lasting impact. So he came down, and we were sitting talking together with another friend, Josh Ewing, who is a missionary to Indonesia now. As we discussed it, Shawn asked me what I would do if I were his age. He was in his early thirties and had a wife and four kids. My answer? "There's no need for me to tell you what I *would* do, I'll tell you what I *did* do."

In 1985, God began to work in my heart. I had pastored and built a church from scratch for eight years. God had blessed, and the church had grown to a respectable size, averaging 175 in attendance. Seventy-five or more were people who drove to church, and many came on our buses. I had been used by God to reach others, but He began to burden my heart and give me a hunger for reaching even more people. Every time a missionary came through my church doors, it caused me to want to be and do something greater than I'd ever done before. As a young man, I dreamed. I read the biographies of Charles Spurgeon and various missionaries. As a country boy working in the fields, I'd look up and see the planes flying, and I'd think to myself, *Someday I wish I could get on one of those airplanes and travel somewhere in the world, and that God would greatly use me.* I dreamed of having the opportunity to preach ten times a week. I dreamed of possibly having Bible colleges where young men and women were trained to carry the gospel message around the world.

I did everything I could while I was a young man in the United States of America. There came a point where I questioned if any of my dreams would come true. I knew I was a very small fish in a very large pond. I heard a famous preacher say if you can't cut it in America, go overseas. So I didn't want to go overseas because my pride caused me to want to stay in America and have people respect me and think highly of me. However, a day came when I died to myself, at least for that moment, and thought I must go overseas. And I did just that.

I completed deputation and, after language school, ended up in Peru. Over the next few years, God allowed me to see every dream I'd ever have come to life. I preached an average of ten times a week, had a Bible college with 125 young men and women, and saw churches started all over our city and country.

Sitting in Josh Ewing's living room, as Shawn asked me what I would do if I were young again, I told him what I did at his age. I told him I'd go to the mission field. There are places all over the world, but my heart would be in Latin America. Can you imagine a place where souls are so receptive? The Roman Catholic Church has brought them so close to knowing about Jesus, but they don't know Him. They know about the Holy Spirit, the Trinity, the Cross, and about the Resurrection, but it hasn't been made personal to them. They have been brought almost, but not fully, to the point of being born again and saved.

I wanted to go somewhere I could preach where so many would be ready to hear the gospel and be saved. I wanted to go where there was a massive harvest ready to be reaped and people waiting to hear the gospel message. I wanted to go to a place where I'd have complete freedom to drive down the streets in a car with a loudspeaker on top and say, "Come to church tonight and hear an international conference speaker from America preach to you from the Word of God." I was that international speaker, and people came and got saved. We would go down to the city market, and one of the guys would get the market speaker and let me preach since I was an American with a funny accent. I would take the microphone and give a brief gospel message to an entire market full of hustling people.

We saw God change lives. We saw terrorists come to Christ who had been a part of the Shining Path Communists' rising against the government. They had spent months in prison, gotten saved, become preachers, and later missionaries. We saw hopeless people receive hope. I remember one Peruvian lady saying to me, "I thank God for the message you give because Jesus gives us our dignity back."

If I were a young person today, I'd go to the mission field. Latin America would be at the top of my radar because it is a place where there are so many people waiting to be saved. It is a place where many young people could be trained and sent out to preach the gospel around the world. A person can legally start a church on every street corner and see God work. What a place where my life could be used to make a change!

Many times, pastors in America become complacent and are satisfied with their ministry because people come together and try to evangelize our community. Sadly, the U.S. is a country that has become hardened to the gospel. Yet I could stand in Arequipa, Peru, and everybody sat on the edge of their seat, wanting to hear more of the gospel instead of less. People were listening to hear the Bible preached. I remember preaching on a Sunday morning and a visitor came who had been to another church. One of the young men in the congregation heard the visitor lean over and ask his wife if she'd ever heard anything like this. The visitor was amazed that I took the Bible and made it come alive. Figuratively speaking, why would you want to maintain an aquarium when you could fish in the deep end of the ocean where thousands of fish are ready to be caught and brought to Jesus? In Latin America, you can truly be a fisher of men.

Training at the Our Generation Training Center (OGTC) is the only thing that is keeping you from going to the mission field. Money is not a problem; you can be taught how to raise the support needed because deputation still works. We can help you overcome the training obstacles you will face. There is an unlimited amount of possibilities. You can start multiple churches. The men who wrote this book have started multiple churches, and they're seeing men saved and lives changed. They are seeing those men go out from their ministry and spread all over the world, preaching the gospel message.

What is your wildest dream? What is your greatest imagination? Young preachers, dream big! If you dream of preaching and of being used of God, this is your opportunity! There is no limit to who you are and what you can do if you would trust God to use you.

Latin America today is in chaos. The truth is that Bolivia's government is currently unstable. The president had to step down because he lost the election overnight and moved to Mexico, saying he is still going to try and affect the election. Venezuela is bankrupt, and their only hope right now is Jesus. Peru, in our day, was shaken by terrorism that killed sixty thousand to seventy-five thousand people over ten years. Chile has had unrest in which over a hundred major stores have been burned and looted. The country is in chaos. Argentina's society is falling apart at this very moment, and Mexico is full of violence due to criminals and drug runners.

Do you realize all the chaos and all the problems in South America may work as a deterrent to going to the mission field, but in actuality, when people are scared and in need is when they're most receptive to the gospel? Right now, Latin America is ripe for harvest. The people are intelligent, good, friendly, loving, and sweet.

If I had one thing to say about my time in Peru, I'd admit two things. First, my skin color could not change to theirs, and second, my tongue could never reflect a Latin heart that beat deep within my chest full of love for the Latin American people who were headed to hell without accepting Christ as their Savior. I want you to think about what will happen when they die without Jesus Christ. They have done the best they know to do. They have gone to Mass, they have followed all the rules, confessed their sin, and yet they will stand before God, and He will say He never knew them. They will say, "Lord, we did what we were told to do. We did what our parents taught us to do, what our priests taught us to do. We thought we could come to heaven!"

They are taught to believe that when they die, their family will be able to pay them out of Purgatory. They have been taught that they will not go to hell, but they will go to a suffering place temporarily and that their family members will get them out. You and I know the truth. We know that there's no way to heaven but through Jesus Christ. We know that the good works they do will not save them and that they will only go to heaven based on what Jesus Christ did. They do not know that. We know Jesus Christ is the only way, the truth, and the life, and that no man comes to the Father except through Him. Yet they believe that the saints may open doors for them, their good works will fix things for them, and that confessing their sins to a priest or giving money will grant them an entrance into heaven. That is not true. What a shame to consider that they are so close and yet so far away!

If I were young again and considering what I want to do, I'd tell myself that there's a place where millions of people are so close to being saved and yet have not trusted Christ. The reason they haven't trusted Christ is that they have a lot of truth but not *the* truth. They have tried to establish their own righteousness as it says in Romans chapter 10, but they need to know that Jesus is the end of the law and that He did it all. On the cross, Jesus said, "It is finished." He meant that literally. It is finished. Jesus paid it all.

So, if I were young again, I'd be a missionary. If I were young again, I'd raise my support, go to the mission field, learn the language, learn the culture, and work with a mission agency that could help me. I'd find a place like the OGTC that could train me, and then I'd go to the mission field and begin leading people to Jesus. I'd start multiple churches. I'd train multiple leaders, start a Bible college, and try to be a part of changing the world. I would dream big dreams.

We were given a command to go into all the world and preach the gospel to every creature. I would take that so seriously. I'd realize that I could easily spend my life where it's comfortable, where I don't have to learn a language or adapt to a new culture, but I would always have in the back of my mind that God could have used me to accomplish so much more. The most exciting life you could ever dream of living, the most wonderful, passionate place to ever be is right on the edge of the battlefield seeing people saved. There is no place anywhere in the world anymore prepared to hear the gospel and be saved than Latin America. From the tip of South America all the way through Mexico, there are people wanting to hear the gospel. Young men will come out of the woodwork and be trained. Jonathan Anderson has been working to reach Cuba, and there's much that needs to be done. You can be a part of that and get involved to be used by God. Currently at Vision, we have no missionaries to Paraguay, Uruguay, Brazil, and others. Why shouldn't you be the first?

I am challenging you as you read this to consider what you should do with your life. What have you been doing? Can you do more by going, or can you do more by staying? Is there a reason for you to be here when He said go and teach all nations? Is there a reason for you to be here when so many are willing to stay, and so few are willing to go? The Bible says in Acts 1:8, "But ye shall receive power, after that the Holy Ghost has come upon you: and ye shall be witnesses unto me..." If we read the New Testament, we'd see a missionary spirit. Initially, we'd read about the first church in Jerusalem, frozen and staying in their country. Eleven chapters into the book of Acts, they are in poverty and have lost what God wanted to do among them. A new church rises among them, and they become the church that God uses. They are the church that carries the gospel to the world and makes a difference.

What will you do with your life? Will you pray about all those countries in the Americas? Will you pray about so many places that need the gospel message? I know you may have heard that they have already been reached, but that's simply not true. There is a need all over the world, but in many parts of the world, it's like chiseling granite to try to get a church started. In Latin America, however, people are coming to Christ. You may have heard that Brazil is the most reached country in the world, but I would say to you we might consider the United States of America and ask about it. You and I both know in America, that not even one county has over 50% attendance on Sunday morning among all denominations. No country in the world is fully reached with the gospel of Christ. In Latin America, there are so many people in such desperate need of the gospel who would listen if they only had a preacher. I believe the Holy Spirit of God is saying, "Who will go for us?"

It is your time to answer and say, "Here am I, send me."

What Led Me To Latin America

<u>*Kyle Shreve*</u>

Why did I choose Latin America? Or why did Latin America choose me?

I think why I chose Latin America, or why anyone should consider it, comes down to a tension between two seemingly opposing truths, God's calling versus human logic.

The first truth is that I believe God called me. There are a million pithy sayings about how to know you're called to preach or called to a certain country.

"You'll just know."

"If you can do anything else, do it. If you can go anywhere else, go."

Just two examples, but you get the idea. But there really is some truth to those statements. I really feel that God has called me to Latin America. Maybe you could classify it as an internal, God-given desire, or maybe something else, but there exists in me a desire to work in Latin America. I can't exactly explain where it came from or how it got there (other than saying it's a calling from God), but it's there.

So on one hand, yes, I DO believe God called me.

On the other hand, it's the most logical choice when you consider the potential to do the most for the cause of world evangelism.

Consider that it is easy to get into almost every country in Latin America, and just as easy to stay. I've never heard of a missionary getting kicked out of Latin America, or having to flee from persecution. While it's not wrong to go to countries where that can happen, and even necessary for someone to go, I don't want to be that person. I think it's wisest to go to a place where, Lord willing, I can spend two or three decades working with minimal governmental interference.

Also consider that we've seen God do incredible things in Latin America in the past five or six decades. Logically, if you have to pick between two fishing spots, would you fish in a pond where there are fewer fish biting and you may get kicked out, or a spot where you can fish as much as you want, as long as you want, and plenty of fish are biting?

Looking at it logically, for me it's a simple choice.

So, on the one hand, I really feel it is God's calling and leading in my life. On the other, it seems like such a logical choice, I would find it hard to pick anywhere else. If you feel a desire and calling for Latin America, then by all means, follow it. If you feel a calling and leading to somewhere else, I would be the last one to stand in the way of your following God's will for your life.

But if you just feel called or desirous of serving as a foreign missionary, and aren't sure where to go or where to start, consider Latin America- the most logical choice.

WHAT NEXT?

As you've read these pages, no doubt your heart has burned with desire to reach Latin America as you've seen testimony after testimony about changed lives. You know there is so much more to be done, and you may wonder what to do next.

The Our Generation Training Center in Alpharetta, Georgia, is a place where you can go to learn about church planting on the mission field. Led by veteran missionary Austin Gardner, the OGTC is where men and women come together to fulfill the Great Commission in our generation.

At the OGTC, you will receive hands-on training and life-on-life mentoring, patterned after the example Jesus gave us with the twelve disciples in the Bible. You have the opportunity to become part of a group of people intent on seeing the world reached with the gospel.

If you're interested in being a church-planting missionary, we hope you'll take the next step by coming to the OGTC. You can feel free to contact one of us and we will put you on the right path.

But whatever you decide, the Scripture is clear that we all have a responsibility to reach Latin America with the gospel. We pray that whether you go yourself or send others, you will always be involved in finishing the task that is set before us.

When our generation passes off the scene, may we not leave the task unfinished.

CONTACT US

Jonathan Anderson - projectwinmexico@gmail.com

Shawn Bateman - batemansinargentina@gmail.com

Robert Becker - rnbmissions@gmail.com

Kason Bloom - kason.bloom@gmail.com

Jeff Bush - jeffmindybush@gmail.com

Stephen Carrier - stephencarrier44@gmail.com

Wayne Cooke - waynelina@gmail.com

Andrew Garcia - ag76nihon@gmail.com

W. Austin Gardner - wagardner@gmail.com

Lauren Grant - laurentoperu@gmail.com

Patrick Henry - phenryj@gmail.com

Jason Holt - holt@biblicalmissions.com

Josh Miller - millerstoperu@gmail.com

Tracy Paver - tracypaver@gmail.com

Miguel Sanabria - sanabmiguel@gmail.com

Kyle Shreve - kyleshreveyoung@gmail.com

Daniel Sparks - sparkstochile@gmail.com

Stephen Underwood - sunderwood52@gmail.com

Kevin White - ktwbmw73@gmail.com

Andrew Wilder - awilder1633@gmail.com

Blake Young - blakeandbridgette@gmail.com

BIBLIOGRAPHY

1. 20 Jim Elliot Quotes: Christian Missionary Quotes from Leadership Resources. (2016, January 20). Retrieved December 20, 2019, from https://www.leadershipresources.org/blog/christian-missionary-jim-elliot-quotes/.

2. Bodenheimer, R. (2019, July 28). What Is Latin America? Definition and List of Countries. Retrieved December 19, 2019, from https://www.thoughtco.com/what-is-latin-america-4691831.

3. Latin America Population 2019. (2019, May 12). Retrieved December 19, 2019, from http://worldpopulationreview.com/continents/latin-america-population/.

4. Masci, D. (2014, November 14). Why has Pentecostalism grown so dramatically in Latin America? Retrieved from https://www.pewresearch.org/fact-tank/2014/11/14/why-has-pentecostalism-grown-so-dramatically-in-latin-america/.

5. Religion in Latin America. (2017, September 7). Retrieved from https://www.pewforum.org/2014/11/13/religion-in-latin-america/.

6. United Nations. (2019). *World Urbanization Prospects. World Urbanization Prospects*(pp. 1–126).

Made in the USA
Monee, IL
02 February 2020

21187352R00085